Ferrari

Godfrey Eaton

Ferrari

Godfrey Eaton

MALLARD
PRESS

Page 1: Phil Hill managed third place at Monaco in 1963 with the 65-degree Dino V6 engine. The 120-degree engines had two separate carburetor grilles.

Pages 2-3: The first production Ferrari with the four-cam V12, the Type 275GTB/4 was announced at the Paris Show in October 1966. The engine produced 300bhp at 8000rpm through six Weber 40 DCN17 carburetors.

Below: Ferrari Testa Rossa V12 from 1958 and Testarossa flat 12 from 1985.

Contents

The Prancing Horse Emblem

For more than four decades the black prancing horse emblem has imprinted the name Ferrari in the minds of those people whose interest in automobiles goes beyond their more mundane use as a means of transportation. It is not difficult to understand why, for Ferrari stands for engine power, for high speed touring and for haut-monde styling. So where does all this fit in with a man who emerged from World War I in poor health with only a scrap of paper given to him by his commanding officer as an introduction to the giant FIAT enterprise for a job which they, in any case, denied him?

Enzo Ferrari had no formal engineering education (he had refused to go to a technical college), but he did have a practical introduction as his father owned a metal and motor business. So even if in his earlier years he had been unable to read a draftsman's design from the drawing board, he probably knew as much about the mechanics of a car as any trained automobile engineer.

It is said that, as a young man, Enzo Ferrari had two ambitions. To become a singer (which he was unlikely to achieve, being tone deaf) and to be a journalist. This latter career he partially fulfilled for, from the time he formed his Scuderia Ferrari in 1929, he would issue yearly 'bulletins' and subsequently annual publications on his organization's progress. And from the time he set up his own factory, in 1946, to build racing and gran turismo cars, he held an annual press conference which was attended by all the leading motor journalists. Ferrari had a keen sense of the press which was not always kind to him but then he was always a man to pursue his own course.

The young Enzo's father would take him to the local circuits whenever a race meeting was held and there can be little doubt that on these occasions the speed, the smell and the dust and danger must surely have fired his enthusiasm and ambition to be not only a racing driver but to plan his future life to become the foremost name in automobile history.

After working with two relatively minor concerns in the motor industry, Ferrari's arrival at the Portobello firm of Alfa Romeo in 1920 was his first major step up the hard road toward his ultimate goal. For a while he formed part of the racing team with two great drivers, Antonio Ascari and Giuseppe Campari, but it was as a co-ordinator and welder of an organization that the company found him most useful.

While the racing of cars was far from becoming a cheap method of keeping a company's name in the forefront it was at the time one of the most effective. To this end Alfa Romeo set up a separate department, to which Ferrari was assigned, with the sole object of being a major contender for grand prix honors.

Ferrari had already persuaded Luigi Bazzi to leave FIAT, which was an astute move, as Bazzi not only remained a close friend and associate of Ferrari during his lifetime but he was to become one of the world's greatest technical engineers sorting out the myriad problems which inevitably arise when a new design takes to the circuits. But Alfa still needed a designer for their grand prix car, as the P1 had been abandoned when Ugo Sivocci had been fatally injured during practice for the 1923 Italian Grand Prix at Monza. Whether it was Ferrari who persuaded Vittorio Jano to leave FIAT, or the Alfa Romeo board, is irrelevant, but there can be little doubt that Ferrari was in the background showing that he was already a man who could pick a particular individual for a particular project. This was an invaluable trait which he never lost.

Ever the opportunist, Ferrari discussed his plans to form his own racing team with two young and wealthy industrialists at an important dinner function. The outcome was the formation in December 1929 of Scuderia Ferrari. The basic idea was to race the Alfa Romeo cars (mainly the sports racing cars) using amateur drivers who would share in any prize money going but would not require professional fees. He was astute enough, however, to hire one professional driver in a move to give status to his team and would also ensure that race promoters would pay start money. It didn't take Ferrari long to realize that amateur drivers did not bring the prestige and money necessary to run a racing team, so he disposed of them. A lot of things went right during the thirties, particularly during the first few years when the com-

Previous pages: A young Ferrari at the wheel of an ES Sport Alfa Romeo before the 1923 Targa Florio. He failed to finish but Ugo Sivocci won in a similar car.

Left: Enzo Ferrari, many years later. The name that has become a legend above all others in automotive circles.

Above: The Prancing Horse, an emblem as Italian as Bolognese sauce.

Right: Over 40 years of Ferrari. A 1948 Tipo 166 Corsa Spyder – one of the first V12s with a 308GTS, one of the most recent V8s.

petition was not all that strong, but things started to go sour with the advent of the two German teams, Mercedes and Auto Union, which had almost unlimited resources. On the other hand Alfa Romeo was pressed for money and while new cars were in evidence their development was undoubtedly restricted. The Scuderia was not without its successes in the major grand prix but it had to rely mainly on income from the less prestigious events. Both Ferrari and Luigi Bazzi became disenchanted and even went so far as to build the two Bi-Motores in 1935 which although highly successful in formula libre were ineligible for the major grands prix. Ferrari had little or no say in what cars should be produced, which must have been more than annoying, but he was permitted to build a team of 1500cc straight-eight cars for voiturette racing, the Alfettas, and was loaned the great Gioacchino Colombo as consultant.

A further blow came in 1938 when the Alfa Romeo board decided to race their cars, forming Alfa Corse. They invited Ferrari to head the team but as he was in constant conflict with the chief engineer, Spaniard Wilfredo Ricart, he quit. Under the severance terms Ferrari was forbidden to build any cars carrying his own name for a period of four years. Also, the Scuderia could not operate for the same period so in the meantime Ferrari set up a new firm, Auto-Avio Construzioni.

It is difficult, once more, to speculate on what Ferrari might have done had not World War II intervened. He was certainly not idle, being a man of activity, and his first venture was to construct, with the help of his 'team' and some outside assistance, two 1500cc eight-in-line sports racing cars. Called 815 Vettura the idea was to enter them for the 1940 Mille Miglia. The construction was based on FIAT parts as that company was offering financial inducements to constructors who used their parts and were successful. The cars did not bear the name Ferrari and he was careful to point out that they had been built for customers.

Ferrari couldn't have had much money at that time but he was building up a business which took off as a result of lucrative contracts manufacturing parts for the war effort. In fact business prospered, enabling him to build much larger premises. In 1946 his new factory was usable even though it had received bomb damage, he had a strong workforce, including an invaluable nucleus who knew about racing cars, and, most important, he knew what he wanted and where he was going. Although the first objective was to build a team of grand prix cars, their initial appearance was delayed until the Italian Grand Prix on 5 September 1948 held over the Valentino Park circuit at Turin. In the meantime three *competizione* or sports racing cars were available by 1947, designated 125 C or 125 S.

While the same basic engine was used for the grand prix and sports racing cars it was not long before there were variations. It is also of note that Colombo's 60 degree V12 unit was the basis of a number of engines, including gran turismo units, right up to 1970-71 when the 5-liter V12 powered the 512 S and M sports racing cars.

Colombo didn't remain long as chief engineer and consultant, as his number two, Aurelio Lampredi had his own ideas which, while not acceptable to Colombo, found favor with Ferrari. There was one thing Ferrari must have wanted almost more than anything else at that stage of his career – to defeat the almost invincible Alfa Romeo 1500cc supercharged straight-eight racing cars. He achieved his objective, not by winning the 1952 formula 1 championship which he narrowly lost, but because Alfa Romeo were in no position to build a new grand prix car and further development of the type 159 was not feasible. Ferrari's 375 Fl unsupercharged 4.5-liter car designed by Lampredi would be top dog. It was unfortunate that the 375 Fl had no 'takers' so formula 1 racing waned until it was revived in 1954.

Apart from formula 1 racing Ferrari was interested and totally involved in sportscar, prototype, and gran turismo racing which, at times, meant he overstretched his resources to the detriment of the cars. This can be noted in a number of tipos which had they been developed further could have become 'winners.' All that can be said is that Ferrari knew his business and what he wanted, and lesser mortals had to keep their views to themselves!

In his 80th year Ferrari decided to change direction and abandoning the flat 12 racing cars produced his 1500cc V6 turbo charged formula 1 car for the 1981 season. Not many men of his age would have bothered to take a new line and although it was said that his enthusiasm for racing had waned, it must have given him great satisfaction to see how well his 'new baby' was doing. Even those motor racing individuals who may not be Ferrari-orientated must surely pay tribute to a man who always upheld the sport of motor racing and who contributed so much toward its progress and continuance.

It is always difficult to look into the future whether it be forecasting the shape or the power pack of the automobile. Apart from current Ferrari formula 1 cars, which use a turbocharger to get extra power from the boost, will the road cars change direction and follow the trends of the formula 1 cars which went turbo in the eighties using composites, multi-valve heads and computers in keeping with racetrack lessons.

Left: One of the very first production Ferraris: a 1947 Tipo 125. Originally with a 1500cc V12 engine, there were soon 1995cc versions. This attractive all-enveloping body was by Carrozzeria Touring.

Right: The 512M contested CanAm – and other prototype races – in 1970 and 1971, but was never really a serious contender. Some of the cars were pitched against Porsche in the European sports-car Championship but again lost out on reliability.

Above: The 1952 Tipo 225 Sport Spyder. Sleek bodywork was designed by Giovanni Michelotti and built by Alfredo Vignale in Turin.

Left: The Tipo 225 came with a 2715cc V12, with a bore and stroke of 70×58.8mm. It revved to 7200rpm and produced 210bhp.

Top right: The car most Ferraristi expect will put the prancing horse on the winner's rostrum in IMSA – the fabulous F40.

Right: No mechanized moving track on the Ferrari production line. No mess nor dirt either. A line of 328s await final inspection.

Sportscars and Sports Racers

In simple terms the dictionary will reveal that the word prototype means 'the first or original type or model from which anything is copied.' However, the interpretation of prototype in this chapter refers to cars built for a specific purpose to conform to regulations for sports racing championship events as laid down by the authorities controlling motor sport. Such cars were manufactured for speed and for endurance races on closed circuits and designed supposedly as a basis for future production models. This being the case, there were two places in the cockpit and a certain amount of equipment which would be necessary should they ever be driven on the open road, all of which was somewhat nonsensical.

While Ferrari had over the years built one-off prototypes, entering them for events for which they would be eligible prior to going into limited production runs, it was not until 1961/62 that he became heavily committed to gran turismo and sportscar prototypes. At that time British constructors had proved conclusively to the racing fraternity that the logical position for the power plant was behind the driver. Now, while Ferrari had shown that he could be flexible and, seemingly without effort, could produce new engines and cars almost at will, he was not totally convinced that the day of the front-engined racing and sports racing car was over, any more than he was convinced that the disk brake was more efficient than the drum brake.

So 1961/62 was to be a turning point with a number of rear or mid-mounted prototypes coming from the factory which were the forerunners not only of the racing cars but more importantly of the sports racing cars, which carried the logo of the prancing horse to frequent championship victories.

The SP Cars

The SPs (Sports Prototypes) were a small but highly important series of V6 and V8 mid-engined cars evolved and developed by Maranello for sportscar racing. Their beginnings are traced back to the regulations set out by the CSI for the new formula 2 racing to become effective in 1957. These stipulated displacement of up to 1500cc unsupercharged with pump fuel to be used in the first year and the higher octane aviation fuel from 1958. There was every prospect of Ferrari participation bearing in mind the highly successful seasons when the 166 F2 and 500 F2 cars reigned supreme.

Ferrari decided on a V6 layout for the new formula and the first car appeared at the Naples Grand Prix on 28 April 1957 where, running out of its class, Luigi Musso placed it third behind the two formula 1 Lancia-Ferraris of Mike Hawthorn and Peter Collins.

Ferrari's son Dino was prominent in the early discussions which influenced Ferrari in adopting the V6 layout and his name became associated with the cars using this engine configuration. His name also prefixed the V8 sports racing cars and continued to be used for the first mid-engined transverse mounted V8 gran turismo car of 1973, the 308 GT4 2 + 2, but his name was 'dropped' from the series in 1976 when the name and all badges were changed to Ferrari.

There have been three series of V6 engines used to power a range of formula 1, formula 2, sports racing and gran turismo cars. Vittorio Jano, the brilliant automobile engineer who joined Ferrari in 1955, when he 'came over' with the Lancia racing department, was responsible for the first two series and Franco Rocchi, the third.

Jano's first effort was the formula 2 V6 engine of 1956/57 which was considered too advanced and complicated for private entrants so in 1959 a second simpler series was introduced.

The third design by Rocchi, in 1965, was also produced for formula 2 racing and at the same time Ferrari was looking for a unit to power a road-going car as the regulations for the formula stipulated that a minimum of 500 had to be built. Franco Rocchi decided to go back to Jano's 1957 design and this was to be one of the most successful designs to come from the factory, as in a variety of displacements it powered the front-engined Fiat Dinos which provided the necessary production basis for the formula 2 cars, a range of mid-engined sports racing prototypes, and the mid-engined Dino 206 GT, Dino 246 GT, and GTS road cars.

At his annual pre-season press conference on 13 February 1961, Ferrari unveiled two new cars, the mid-engined Dino 156 1500cc formula 1 contender and his prototype replacement for the 250 Testa Rossa series which had served him well in the sports racing championships. The new car was the now famous Dino 246 SP mid-engined sports racing car. For both cars designer and engineer Chiti had adapted the Jano 1956/57 Dino engine derived from the 2.5-liter formula 1 cars.

Previous pages: The 206 SP Dino had an unusual 65 degree V6 engine, putting out some 240bhp from 1986cc.

Left: Ferrari entered three cars for Le Mans in 1958. This is the Hawthorn/Collins entry which recorded the fastest lap of 4m 8s at 121.3mph before retiring with a burnt-out clutch.

Right, top and bottom: More of the 1966 206 SP Dino. From front and rear, it has beautiful curvy lines reminiscent of the 330 P3.

Body styling was entirely new for a Ferrari and while not as attractive as the Testa Rossa, it had a purposeful look which meant business. The design had been evolved after Chiti had persuaded Ferrari to install a wind-tunnel. It was hightailed from the back of the cockpit with a headrest fairing which ended in a sharp-edged form at the Kamm-type tail. The body design had a shortish nose and incorporated twin-nostrils which had been copied from a design by Fantuzzi.

Before the Sebring 12-hour race Richie Ginther was given the job of testing the works sports racing cars and found that the high rear deck was causing instability. Ginther, who had connections with the aircraft industry, solved the problem after trial and error by having a type of spoiler tacked to the lip of the car's tail. This cured the poor handling but at the same time dropped the car's speed.

A second car was ready in time for the Targa Florio run on 30 April over the

Madonie circuit. Von Trips and Ginther drove the Sebring car while Phil Hill and Gendebien had the new one. Phil Hill, trying to make up time after a start line fiasco involving his co-driver, did considerable damage to the front end of his car. However, von Trips retrieved the day for Ferrari by taking his car first over the line and he also set a new lap record of 67.01mph.

For the Le Mans 24-hour race on 10-11 June the factory entered only one Dino 246 SP for Ginther and von Trips but von Trips ran out of fuel on the Mulsanne straight – a bad pit blunder! All was not lost for Maranello as the Phil Hill/Gendebien combination won in the TR1/61 (V12 Testa Rossa) and gave the Scuderia its seventh World Championship Sports Car title.

There was a trauma at the factory during the winter of 1961 when a major row broke out when Romolo Tavoni (team manager), Carlo Chiti (chief engineer), and other highly placed personnel walked out. While Ferrari might have been distressed up to a point it has always been widely known that to

him machines were of greater importance than men and there were others to take the place of those who left. True, development work was interrupted but Chiti had not been idle before his departure and Ferrari still had something to show at his 1962 press conference on 24 February. There were three new mid-engined sports racing cars on view, all of which looked alike externally, so it was just as well that the factory had taken the trouble to paint on each its type number. They were all Dinos and the smallest capacity car was the under 2-liter 196 SP introduced originally in 1958 as a customer 196 S sports racing car with a V6 engine. This engine was carried on in the 196 SP but with an increase in power to 210bhp at 7500rpm and a 5-speed transmission. Also in the line-up was the new Dino 286 SP with a swept volume of 2862cc. The engine was based on the original Chiti 60 degree 'half-V12' block. The compression ratio was 9.5:1 and the unit produced 260bhp at 6800rpm. Perhaps of greater interest to those present were two Dino 248 SPs developed by Chiti with 90 degree V8 units and with a displacement of 2458.7cc. The engine could be readily enlarged using a new crankshaft which increased the displacement to 2644.9cc and in this larger form the Dino 268 SP was rated at more than 260bhp at 7500rpm. All of these Dinos were sufficiently 'simple' to be sold to various teams who would find no difficulty in maintaining them. For 1961 the FIA had decreed a minimum height for windshields which displeased both constructors and drivers but this somewhat arbitrary rule was dropped for 1962 and the rear decks of the new Dino SPs were lowered giving each car a far more handsome appearance.

The Daytona Speedway saw the first major sportscar race for the 1962 season on 11 February. Two Ferraris appeared for the 3-hour race with Phil Hill partnering Ricardo Rodriguez in a revised-bodied 246 SP which was entered by Ricardo's father, while Luigi Chinetti's NART entered a 246 S for Buck Fulp who also shared his car with Rodriguez. Although Hill had set the pace a slow driver change-over cost him the race in which he finished second to Dan Gurney in a sick Lotus 19. Fulp was eighth. After Hill and Gendebien had taken first place at Nurburgring in a 246 SP the 196 SP was given a new role and was handed over to Scuderia Sant' Ambroeus for Ludovico Scarfiotti to drive in the European Mountain Championship with Dragoni supervising. Generally speaking the event had been a preserve of the Porsches which was to be shattered in 1962. The 196 SP missed the first round but ran at the Fornovo-Monte Cassio climb on 10 June establishing a new record and beating four Porsches. A week later at Mont Ventoux the Porsche factory entered a

2-liter flat 8 spyder but it made no difference as the 196 SP smashed Maurice Trintignant's 1960 record by the huge margin of 24 seconds for the 13.4 mile climb. 8 July saw the 'circus' gather for the 10.75 mile climb at Trento-Bondone but once again Scarfiotti took the honours and on the resurfaced road collected a new record, reducing the time by an incredible 45 seconds. Scarfiotti blew off the Porsches again on 22 July when the 196 SP set another hill climb record and the aggregate of the two runs bettered the closest Porsche by a fraction over 10 seconds. The unexpected happened at Ollon-Villars on 25 August when Scarfiotti was 0.2 seconds behind Sepp Greger's RS 1700 after two runs, no doubt due to running on two new and unscrubbed front tyres. This event clinched the title for Scarfiotti and the 196 SP so it was decided to forgo the final event.

Le Mans, to be run on 23-24 June, showed a great diversification of cars entered by works and privateers. There were 15 Ferraris including 250 TR, 250 GT special, 250 short wheelbase, 250 GTO and GTO special. The works cars consisted of the surviving 268 SP for Baghetti/Scarfiotti, a 246 SP for the Rodriguez brothers while Mike Parkes and co-driver Bandini had a 330 LM berlinetta. The 268 SP had been running well when transmission problems caused its retirement in the 18th hour. Meanwhile the Rodriguez brothers had been swapping the lead with Hill and Gendebien for 12 hours but were also sidelined with transmission troubles. Despite these set-backs Hill and Gendebien continued on their way to take first overall. Their car was designated by the works as 330TR/LM and powered by the 4-liter V12 400 Superamerica engine. It was a spyder and also sported the full rear deck width airfoil section behind the driver. These sections were known affectionately as 'basket handles'!

An interesting development and the whole purpose of the 'SP exercise' came together late in 1962 when a V12 unit was slipped into a 246 SP chassis. The car was tested at Modena and Monza with John Surtees at the wheel. The new concept certainly made its mark as Surtees proceeded to break Ginther's Monza lap record.

The 250 P

The car with which John Surtees broke Ritchie Ginther's lap record at Monza in November 1962 was the development model for the 250 P which Ferrari had on show at his press conference in March 1963. The original chassis was from a 246 SP but it had been 'stretched' to accommodate a V12 250 Testa

Above left and left: Swoopy 248 SP came with a sohc V8 of 2458.7cc capacity. Unveiled early in 1962, its competitive life was cut short after Stirling Moss rejected it in favor of a 3-liter Testa Rossa at Sebring. This lack of power was partially cured by fitting a bigger 2644.9cc engine, though the 268 SP (right) kept the same bodywork. Phil Hill drove the 268 SP at the 1962 Targa Florio but wrote the car off in practice.

Right: An 801 Dino at the 1957 British Grand Prix at Aintree. Ferrari entered four cars, with drivers Mike Hawthorn, Peter Collins, Maurice Trintignant and Luigi Musso.

Left: One of the three 1963 Le Mans 250 P entries. This one, the Bandini/Scarfiotti entry, went on to win after the leading Surtees/Mairesse entry crashed at 4am.

Right: The 250 LM was supposed to take over from the old 250 GTO as the first Ferrari rear-engined 'GT' car, but homologation never materialized.

Below: The Ferrari garage at Le Mans in 1963 shows line of works 250 P3s.

Rossa engine – virtually the 3-liter unit with six 38 DCN Weber carburetors and dry sump lubrication. It was taken to the 1963 Targa Florio as a 'training' car but after a fuel line breakage it was severely damaged by fire.

The single overhead camshaft 3-liter V12 was rated at 300bhp at 7800rpm with six Weber carburetors and a compression ratio of 9.8:1.

Suspension was independent all round using double wishbones and concentric shock absorbers with coil springs. The disk brakes were placed inboard at the rear on either side of the transaxle assembly.

Under the hood could be found the oil tank for the dry sump lubrication, a radiator for oil cooling and the water radiator. The spyder bodywork was styled by Pininfarina and the Chiti nose, as seen on the SP series, was abandoned but the 'basket-handle' retained. It was compact and businesslike.

The 250 P contested the Sebring 12-hour on 23 March 1963 when two cars were entered. John Surtees, having his first race for the Scuderia, partnered by Lodovico Scarfiotti, placed their car first having covered some 209 laps. Second home was the other 250 P driven by Willy Mairesse and Nino Vaccarella. Third place was also filled by a Ferrari – the 1962 Le Mans winning car, the NART TR/61, handled by Graham Hill and Pedro Rodriguez and the next three cars home were 250 GTOs which also took 13th, 14th, and 18th places. Quite a triumph for Ferrari, only to be topped in April, during the Le Mans trials, when Surtees lapped the circuit at 133mph clipping no less than 11.6 seconds from the lap record.

While the 250 P had only won two out of the three races so far contested there can be no doubt that Ferraris were on the crest of a wave and demonstrated their superiority once again during the 24-hour Le Mans endurance race on 15-16 June. The cars entered by the Scuderia were a mixed but interesting collection and there can be little doubt that Enzo Ferrari was determined to make every effort to win his fourth Le Mans race in a row. The 250 Ps were in the hands of Surtees/Mairesse, Mike Parkes/Maglioli, and Scarfiotti/Bandini. There were four 330 LMs for the Americans Dan Gurney/Jim Hall, the Englishmen Jack Sears/Mike Salmon, and the Frenchmen Noblet/Guichet while Masten Gregory and David Piper had a similar 3-liter car. Beurlys and Langlois had the fast, reliable 250 GTO as did Elde/Dumay.

Scarfiotti and Bandini won at an average speed of 118.5mph with the 250 GTO taking second overall and first in the GT class at 112.5mph. Following the GTO was another 250 P (Parkes/Maglioli) with the second GTO fourth. To round off this astounding parade of Ferraris the 330 LM of Sears/Salmon was fifth and the 3-liter berlinetta handled by Gregory and Piper sixth.

The 250 Ps had not finished their season as Pedro Rodriguez drove the NART car into second place at the Bridgehampton Double 500 on 15 September and followed this up a week later at the Canadian Grand Prix for sportscars held at Mosport which he won. Early December was 'cocktail time' at the Nassau Speed Week but Rodriguez once again acquitted himself quite well by coming in second in the Nassau Trophy and also the Governor's Cup, making 1963 a year to be remembered as the first rear-engined V12s showed their tails to most of the competitors. The 250 P was Ferrari's venture into the rear-engined V12 cars which he had every intention of marketing as gran turismos.

The 250 LM

Introduced at the Paris Salon in October 1963 the 250 berlinetta Le Mans was to all intents a 250 P with a roof, a vertical rear window with sail panels which tapered into the rear deck, and an air slot at the back in an effort to reduce any turbulence at the cut-off. Ferrari had intended the car as the gran turismo version and the general specification was similar to that of the 250 P. Some modifications were made to the bodywork as the model moved on to the London, Turin, and Brussels shows. The roof line was less angular and had been lengthened and an air intake was let into the forepart of the rear fender to duct cool air to the brakes and carburetors: later this scoop was slightly enlarged but served only the brakes as the carburetors were fed cool air from the rear deck. It was a delightful-looking car with a short nose, beautifully contoured rear fenders and a slightly upturned tail across the back of the rear deck.

Ferrari had hopes that the CSI would homologate the tipo for gran turismo racing but they wouldn't agree as there was a certain looseness in the regulations which other constructors thought should be tightened up. Throughout his long battle with CSI, Ferrari continued to refer to the tipo as a 250 LM and never accepted that it was, in fact, a 275 LM, giving the 40 or so cars which were built odd chassis numbers, a further indication that they were gran turismo cars as far as he was concerned.

Most of the cars were sold to customers and concessionaires who raced them with some success in 1964 with 10 major and many minor wins.

The 275 P and 330 P

For 1964 two new competition models (both spyders) were introduced – the 275 P with specifications similar to the 250 LM, and the 330 P, also with similar specifications to the 250 LM. Six Weber carburetors, 5-speed transmission in unit with the differential, single overhead camshaft per bank of cylinders, a single plug per cylinder and coil ignition offered a power rating of 370bhp at 7300rpm. Coachwork was in essence similar in each prototype to that of the 250 P, but there were varying treatments to individual cars and in some cases the 275 Ps were just re-engined versions of the 250 P.

Neither car appeared until the Sebring 12-hour event on 21 March with the 3.3-liter versions in the hands of Parkes/Maglioli and Vaccarella/Scarfiotti and the 4-liters with Surtees/Bandini, Graham Hill/Bonnier, and Rodriguez/Fulp driving. The Parkes/Maglioli car won at an average speed of 92.4mph with second place going to the 3.3-liter of Vaccarella/Scarfiotti. Surtees and Bandini took third place but the Maranello Concessionaires entry of a 4-liter prototype retired in the ninth hour with transmission failure after being in second place. A hose pipe burst on the Rodriguez/Fulp car in the third hour causing overheating and a necessary retirement.

Next on the calendar was the Nurburgring 1000km held on 31 May when the Scuderia sent the 3.3-liter 275 Ps feeling that these cars would be more suitable to the circuit. Scarfiotti and Vaccarella won at an average speed of 87mph while the Parkes/Guichet GTO was second overall and first in the gran turismo class.

A large contingent of Ferraris contested the Le Mans 24-hour event on 20-21 June including 275 Ps and 330 Ps. Once more a 275 P took the chequered flag with Vaccarella and Guichet driving at an average speed of 121.6mph. Graham Hill and Bonnier in a 330 P came second averaging 119.7mph and another 330 P driven by Bandini/Surtees was next home at 117.3mph. Ferraris also filled the 5th, 6th, 9th, and 16th positions, making the classic endurance race little more than a procession of Ferraris.

Enzo Ferrari had every reason to feel elated with the accomplishments of his competition cars during the 1964 season. The GTOs had won the Manufacturers' Championship, the 275 P and 330 P prototypes were unbeatable, and the 250 LMs had come to good.

Above: A 1955 250 LM from the collection of the Midland Motor Museum, Bridgenorth. A privately-entered 250 LM won Le Mans that year in the hands of Gregory and Rindt.

Above right: A NART (North American Racing Team) private entry 250 LM with rare hardtop in 1965.

Right: The 1964 Le Mans of Surtees and Bandini. The 4-liter car dominated for most of the race, but finished third behind Graham Hill/Bonnier with Vaccarella/Guichet taking the win.

The 275 P2, 330 P2, 365 P2 and 365 P2/3

Ford had entered the European endurance competition scene with the Ford GT40 and its derivatives, and Ferrari was well aware of the threat to his dominance in the prototypes and gran turismo events, so he countered with the 275 P2, 330 P2, 365 P2, and 365 P2/3 for the 1965 season. The first two models were basically for works use while the last two, being less complicated, were for concessionaires and privateers to race.

The P2 prototypes were quite new with the semi-monocoque chassis and the independent rear suspension derived from the formula 1 car. The bodywork for these spyder prototypes was developed from wind-tunnel studies and was not designed by Pininfarina. They were lower, with a more pleasing and sleeker line than the previous prototypes. The nose was nearer to the ground and to prevent any tendency to lift at high speed diplane spoilers were incorporated on either side of the nose. While the first car was fitted with a wraparound screen the later cars were given higher windshields and behind the driver the now familiar 'basket-handle' roll bar. Since the cars were so low to the ground it was necessary to have a bulge on the rear deck to cover the stack of the six twin-choke Weber carburetors atop the 4-liter V12 powerplant, based on an old design developed for the 1957 sportscars.

The first P2 spyder was the 330 with a 4-liter engine while the 275 P2 would use the 3.3-liter engine. For customers the 4-liter 330 P2 engine was bored out to 4.4-liters and the cars were designated 365.

Ferrari refused to enter his new prototypes for the Sebring 12-hour event. He was at loggerheads with the organizers who had included Appendix C sportscars which were powered by the big American engines. A number of private Ferraris were entered, 250 LMs, 275 Ps, 330 Ps, and a GTO, and the only one in the money (3rd place) was the 250 LM in the hands of David Piper and Tony Maggs.

10-11 April was Le Mans trial time and by then the Scuderia had a fully developed 330 P2 on hand for Surtees who proceeded to crack the existing lap record with a blistering 139.9mph, timed down the Mulsanne straight at around 190mph.

There was a big turn out of 14 Ferraris at Monza for the 1000km race but this was to be expected as it was their home ground. Parkes and Guichet took the 275 P2 to victory at an average of 126mph while Surtees and Scarfiotti had to be content with second place as they were plagued with tire trouble, although they were the fastest car and set the quickest lap at 133.7mph. Ferrari used the race to introduce the new Dino 166 P, a 65 degree V6 with twin overhead camshafts per cylinder block and a capacity of 1.6-liters. Baghetti and Giampiero Biscaldi had the drive but went out on lap 1 with engine trouble.

The next endurance event was the Nurburgring 1000km when the Monza result was reversed with Surtees/Scarfiotti taking the chequered flag in the 330 P2 with the 275 P2 of Parkes/Guichet following them home. The Dino 166 P now driven by Bandini/Vaccarella took fourth place although it had

held third position at one stage. As there was some suspicion that the Dino's capacity was greater than alleged (obviously due to its good performance) Eugenio Dragoni (Ferrari team manager) had the engine taken down to be measured, thereby proving its displacement was 1596cc.

On 19-20 June it was once again time for the classic Le Mans 24-hour race but although Ferrari recorded their sixth win in a row it was the privateers who made this possible as all the works cars went out.

Across the Atlantic the Bridgehampton Double 500 was run on 19 September and Pedro Rodriguez managed a second in the NART 365 P2 and Bob Grossman had a fourth place in his 330 P. The race was won by a Chaparral and third spot went to a Cobra. On the same day David Piper was at Mont Tremblant, Quebec, taking part in a 200 miler. He was second in his 365 P2 while Surtees won driving his own Chevrolet-engined Lola 70.

Unfortunately for the factory, the 330 P2 did not perform up to expectations so further work was necessary before the start of the new season in 1966. Nevertheless the other prototypes had done more than enough in the events which counted for Ferrari to take the Prototype title.

The 330 P3

The 330 P3 was a natural development of the 330 P2 and had a number of refinements, mechanical, chassis, and bodywork, in the hope that its competition history would be an improvement over its predecessor's. The engine was the same 4-liter V12 unit but Lucas indirect fuel injection was installed and with the compression ratio raised from 9.5:1 to 11.4:1 the output was increased to 420bhp at 8000rpm. The clutch had been moved so that it was now between the engine and the 5-speed ZF transmission which replaced the Ferrari transmission. There was some revision to the chassis which still followed the formula 1 practice, being made from alloy sheeting, steel tubing, and some fiberglass pieces bonded together. Bodywork was also revised and the overall dry weight had been reduced to a useful 1588 pounds. With FIA rules changed as regards height and width of the windshield, a fairly wide choice was permitted and this suited Ferrari as it was molded, on both spyder and berlinetta versions, to give a smooth line from the front hood which obviously helped in decreasing the overall frontal area to assist windflow. The nose was very low, but not quite as low as the circuit sweepers of the seventies and eighties, with the radiator inlet across the full width. Head lamps, driving lamps, and indicator lamps were clustered in a single plastic cover which was faired-in to the ends of each front wing. The line on the berlinetta from the rear of the driving compartment was smooth with good visibility through the rear windshield. The tail had a small airfoil and a high Kamm-type cut-off. Both spyders and berlinetta were beautifully proportioned with a height of only 38.8 inches, a width of 70 inches and length of 164 inches, and the works claimed a top speed in excess of 190mph.

The 330 P3 made its debut on 26 March for the Sebring 12-hour race, in the hands of Parkes and Bondurant. For some time the car, in spyder body-

Left: John Surtees leads the Bucknum Ford GT 40 at the 1965 Le Mans 24 hours, but gearbox trouble led to the retirement of the Surtees/Scarfiotti team.

Right: The 330 P3; one of two new cars for the 1966 season. It retained a 3967cc V12, rated at 420bhp at 8000rpm. Ferrari entered two twin-overhead-cam per bank 4-liter P3s at Le Mans that year, but the race was a disaster for them.

work, held first or second place but went out in the final hour with a broken gear-selector lever. The Ford menace was growing as their GT Mk2s again ran out in first, second, and third places but the 330 P3 claimed its first victory at the Monza 1000km on 25 April. Run in pouring rain, with day turned to night, the race average speed by the winners was 103.1mph and they also went on to complete the fastest lap at 109.2mph.

Spa-Francorchamps hosted the next round of the championship, again a 1000km race, on 22 May. Parkes and Scarfiotti again shared a 330 P winning at the high average speed of 131.7mph and they also set a new course lap record of 139mph. For the first time a Ferrari works car had been fitted with Firestone tires. The 2-liter class was won by a Dino 206 S berlinetta with Guichet and Attwood driving.

Once more rain fell during an endurance race; on this occasion it was the Nurburgring 1000km held on 5 June. This event gave the 2-liter Dinos a chance to show their real mettle for the Scarfiotti/Bandini car took second place right up the tail of the winning Chaparral 2D coupe (Phil Hill/Jo Bonnier) averaging 89.1mph against the winners' average of 89.4mph. Rodriguez/Richie Ginther, also Dino 206S mounted, were third. The 330 P3, although making fastest lap at 98.6mph in the hands of Surtees, went out on lap 36, the clutch burning out. Transaxle trouble saw the end of the Maranello Concessionaires Dino 206S on lap 28.

The Le Mans classic on 18-19 June was a Ferrari debacle. There were labor problems at the factory so preparation of the cars after the Nurburgring race was minimal and, as if that wasn't enough, Surtees was dumbfounded when he discovered that Scarfiotti was down to share the drive of his 330 P3; he had only expected to have Parkes as co-driver. Team manager Dragoni explained this was a precaution as he felt that Surtees had not recovered fully from injuries sustained during practice for the 1965 Canadian Grand Prix. A furious Surtees stormed off to see Ferrari at Modena leaving the Scuderia without their ace driver. For team discipline Ferrari had to uphold Dragoni's decision which was a pity for it had been Dragoni's attitude to Phil Hill earlier

in the sixties which had made Hill decide to quit. For the race Ferrari fielded three 330 P3s, two Dino 206Ss were entered by NART, and Maranello Concessionaires had one Dino for Salmon/Hobbs.

Four Ferraris had lasted up to the 18th hour but two hours later only two were keeping the marque flag aloft, one finishing 8th overall and first in the GT class, while the other finished in 10th spot.

Ford had, at last, achieved two goals — winning at Le Mans and, perhaps just as important to them, beating Ferrari on what had become their own preserve; at the same time clinching the Manufacturers' Championship with 38 points (two ahead of Ferrari) while Porsche took the Prototype title. Ferrari did not contest any other race with the 330 P3s for the remainder of the season, as no title points were at stake but the other prototypes were still in contention.

1966 had been a season of mixed fortunes for the marque and it must have hurt Ferrari when the Le Mans race was wrested from him, although he could with some justification lay the blame on the industrial unrest which had gripped Italy at the crucial time. There was no point in looking back so Ferrari set out on the trail once more to regain his supremacy over the Ford Motor Company.

The 330 P4

To prepare adequately for the 1967 season Ferrari took his new offering to Daytona for extensive practice. Parkes, Scarfiotti, Chris Amon (a new recruit to the Scuderia), and Bandini were given the job of testing and after a total of 580 laps they called it a day. The Daytona lap record was broken time after time and a top speed of around 210mph had been reached. The car was the 330 P4 with spyder bodywork.

The V12 4-liter engine to power the car was a new design based on an all new formula 1 3-liter unit designed by Ing. Franco Rocchi which had taken the first two places in the 1966 Italian Grand Prix held at Monza. The engine in 3-liter form developed 380bhp at 10,000rpm.

Above left: The 1966 Le Mans marked a clash between Ford and Ferrari that badly bruised the Italians' ego. This is the Bandini/Guichet 330 P3 which retired after 17 hours with a blown head gasket.

Above: The 330 P4, produced for the 1967 season. It was a totally new design, even though it resembled the P3.

Right: A 330 P4 engine. 60-degree V12, 3967cc and 450bhp at 8000rpm were the quoted figures. Note the twin distributors and four coils.

The 4-liter 60 degree V12 had twin overhead camshafts per bank of cylinders with three valves per cylinder, two inlet, and one exhaust. Oil was pushed through the engine and scavenged by two pumps and thence through a chassis frame member to an oil cooler across the front of the car and returned via another chassis frame tube. Water for cooling was also taken from and returned to the radiator via chassis frame tubes.

Suspension was independent all round with transverse wishbones, coil springs with shock absorber units, and anti-roll bars. Brakes were ventilated disk-mounted outboard and cooled by air taken by large bore trunking from scoops in the doors and from slots on either side of the nose.

Two Scuderia 330 P4s were sent to the States for the Daytona 24-hour event to be held on 4-5 February. The spyder, which had been tested so thoroughly on the circuit the previous December, was entrusted to Chris Amon and Bandini while Parkes and Scarfiotti had a new berlinetta. Like Indianapolis a rolling start was used and as the pace maker pulled off Phil Hill in a Chaparral led off but after 3 hours, hit a retaining wall and was out, while the 7-liter Ford Mk2s (of which there were six) all had transmission failures. The factory Ferraris only had minor troubles and at the finish toured the last three laps allowing the NART car driven by Rodriguez/Guichet to join them to cross the finish line abreast.

Ford had lost round one.

Once again on their home ground at Monza on 25 April the first cars home after 1000kms were the 330 P4s of Amon/Bandini and Parkes/Scarfiotti, both sets of drivers using their Daytona cars. All told 17 Ferraris had started from a total entry of 41 which at least gave them good odds!

Ford was still smarting from the debacle at Daytona and was determined to retain the 'crown' they had worked so hard to win at the 1966 Le Mans. This year they entered four new Mk4s and three older Mk2s with engine specifications similar to the Mk4. Ferrari sent three 330 P4s (2 berlinettas and one spyder). He also loaned a 330 P4 to Equipe National Belge for Beurlys/Mairesse. Thirty pounds had been shaved from the weight by using magnesium cases for the 5-speed transmissions. NART, Maranello Concessionaires, and Scuderia Filipinetti had their 330 P3/4 but with the new Ferrari 5-speed transmission. Filipinetti also entered a 2-cam 275 GTB and Chinetti's NART also had the long-tailed 365 P2/3.

For three hours Ford and Chaparral fought out the lead with the Ferrari holding back. At midnight the Parkes/Scarfiotti 330 P4 had moved into third place behind two Fords, but by 3 am the A J Foyt Ford was miles ahead of them. By 2 pm Parkes/Scarfiotti and Beurlys/Mairesse started to motor in earnest, reducing Foyt's lead by 10 seconds every lap, but the chase was useless. All the Fords, Chaparral and Aston Martin Lola were timed down the Mulsanne straight at 200mph or over while the 330 P4s could only muster 193mph.

Still, the final round for the Manufacturers' Championship took place on 30 July at Brands Hatch for the BOAC 500, and this race would decide whether Porsche or Ferrari (with respectively 32 and 31 points) would take the title, since Ford had only 22 points. Ferrari sent three 330 P4 spyders, Maranello Concessionaires entered their 330 P3/4 and there were three 250 LMs, all privately owned. After four hours the Phil Hill/Mike Spence Chaparral was in the lead with the McLaren/Siffert Porsche second and Chris Amon

in the 330 P4 third. Taking advantage of the Porsche pit stop to change brake pads Amon slipped into second place and stayed there to clinch the championship for Ferrari by 2 points.

This was not the end of the Prototypes, except for the prototypes title, as Chinetti's NART car was returned to the factory to be reworked and made lower as it was the intention to run in the CanAm series (first started in 1966). But with only 4 liters against the 7-liter Chevrolet V8 Group 7 cars, it was rather a long shot.

The 312 P

Ferrari decided that he would enter the Manufacturers' Championship for 1969 and introduced his contender, the 312 P, during December 1968. It was a beautiful-looking sports racing spyder resembling a scaled-down version of the 612 CanAm car.

The 2990cc V12 engine had double overhead camshafts per bank of cylinders, 4 valves per cylinder, a single plug, coil ignition. Lucas fuel injection and with a compression ratio of 11.0:1 the power output was 430bhp at 9800rpm. The 5-speed transmission was in unit with the differential. Suspension was independent all round with double wishbones and coil springs. Unlike the CanAm cars the championship prototypes had to be fitted with headlamps; they were set low and faired-into the front fenders.

The 312 P missed out on the Daytona 24-hour but a single entry contested the Sebring 12-hour driven by Amon and Mario Andretti. It made pole position and was leading after 3 hours but then had cooling problems and dropped to second place where it finished the race.

Next seen at the April Le Mans trials it did not live up to its initial debut at Sebring and could only muster a fifth fastest. After this disappointing trial it was expected at Le Mans for the race in June with a berlinetta body.

At Brands Hatch for the 500-miler a lone 312 P lined up in the center of the front row of the grid. At the wheel, Amon led for the first four laps before being passed by Siffert's Porsche. Thereafter he ran in third place until a puncture relegated him to fourth.

Before Le Mans the factory was testing a smooth-outline berlinetta 312 P. It had a long sloping roof with slats over the rear deck and proved very fast in tests. Two of these appeared at Le Mans for Amon/Schetty and Piper/Rodriguez but bad luck and a transmission malfunction put them out.

The 312 Ps were never raced again by the factory as Ferrari pulled out of the Watkins Glen and Austrian events. They were cars which always seemed to flatter only to deceive but perhaps if the works had run a full team of three cars the results might have been better. On the other hand the larger displacement Porsche 917s were reliable, apart from being fast, although the difference in speeds was not great. In any case Ferrari had already set to work to build the 512 S cars to counter the German opposition.

Previous pages: A 1967 330 P4. Only three 'true' P4s were ever built. They were 164.8 inches long and only 39.4 inches high.

Left: A 365 P2, one of the special 'private entry' cars, built in 1965 and rebuilt at Maranello in 1966 with 4.4-liter engines.

Below: Chris Amon rounds Mulsanne Corner in his 330 P4 spider speciale which he shared with Nino Vaccerella in 1967.

The 312 PB

These cars were designed to conform with the regulations of 3 liters for prototypes effective 1 January 1972. Being flat 12s their engine configuration can be traced back to 1964 when the factory introduced a 1.5-liter flat 12 formula 1 car. And while not exactly side-lining these boxer units it was not until the winter of 1969/1970 that the first flat 3-liter formula 1 car, the 312 B, was tested. The 312 PB sports racing car followed, and during tests in October 1970 it was given an aluminum body, this being easy to work on should any revision be necessary. When the time came to take to the circuits a fiberglass body was used. In early races there were no headlamps but these were added in time for the 1971 Sebring 12-hour race.

The 312 PB was really no more than a thinly disguised flat 12 formula 1 racing car but with equipment added necessary for sportscar racing! Tuned for endurance racing and with a compression ratio of 11.5:1 the power output was 450bhp at 11,000rpm which was some 30bhp less than the formula 1 car. The chassis was the usual tubular steel structure covered with sheet aluminum. Bodywork was in two sections and the front portion included the doors. The nose opening was to help keep the front end down and the two ducts on either side of this opening led cool air to the brakes. The water radiators were placed in the center of the chassis on either side of the cockpit and cooled by air intakes recessed in the doors. The oil radiator was atop the engine with two scoops on the rear deck and a larger slot feeding air to the engine compartment. On the 1972 models a low-placed airfoil stretched the width of the tail supported by two struts in a central position and held at the ends by two fins on the edges of the rear fenders. The wheels were slotted alloy disk type.

A single car was sent to Buenos Aires for the opening round of the Manufacturers' Championship in January 1971 with Giunti/Merzario as drivers. During practice it qualified for the front row of the grid and led off the line for five laps until Giunti crashed into a stationary Matra; the Ferrari burst into flames. Giunti died from severe burns and head injuries and the car was wrecked beyond repair.

Jackie Ickx (a new driver for the Scuderia) and Andretti placed their 312 PB on the front row alongside the 5-liter 512 M of Donohue/Hobbs for the Sebring 12-hour. The 312 PB led for most of the first six hours when transmission failure put it out of contention.

Next race was the Brands Hatch 1000km and Ickx/Regazzoni had it on pole. Unfortunately, while in the lead, it took to the grass taking avoiding action from a spinning car. Ten valuable minutes had been lost and despite some quick laps the car was still some three laps in arrears of the winning Alfa Romeo.

Somehow the 312 PB was having little luck, for at the Monza endurance race a third accident put the car out of the race. Ickx had made the front row again and led from the line but on lap 13 he hit wreckage from a Porsche 907.

The accident rate continued on the fast Spa Francorchamps circuit. Although the 312 PB could not match the speed of the 5-liter Gulf Porsches it was running a comfortable third when a slower driver in front of Regazzoni (who was travelling at around 180mph) decided to cut across his line. Result – another retirement.

The Targa Florio was given a miss but the repaired car from Spa appeared at the Nurburgring for the 1000km race. Ickx put the 312 PB on pole and was well into the lead before the half-way mark. But the engine was overheating and it was found that the cylinder heads had cracked. Ferrari decided to miss Le Mans (the 512 S and Ms represented the factory) and go for the Austrian race at the Osterreichring. The Porsches were off song so Ickx and Regazzoni were a good lap ahead of the chasing field after three quarters distance, but once again a race was lost as Regazzoni clouted a guard rail at a turn.

For the final championship round at Watkins Glen, Andretti shared the 312 PB with Ickx. This time the car was relegated to the second row but the beautifully turned out Penske 512M (Donohue/Hobbs) had pole. After a few laps the 312 PB was running second (the Porsches again having an off day) but on lap 54 found itself in the lead for two laps. But, after a scheduled pit stop, the starter motor decided to call it a day with an inevitable retirement.

The results, championship-wise, were not satisfactory but the 312 PB had been proving itself all season and unless something drastic went wrong it looked all set to regain the manufacturers' crown in 1972 when the prototypes' capacity would be 3 liters.

There was to be an all-out assault for the Manufacturers' title in 1972. Peter Schetty was appointed team manager and a further six cars were to be built so that while four (3 for each race and a spare) 312 PBs would be dispatched for each event another four would be at the factory preparing for the next event. Apart from their other factory commitments Ickx and Regazzoni would be a part of the team personnel.

The new car had 445bhp available, was light and very maneuverable. The competition was to come from Alfa Romeo, Mirage, and Matra but the latter only contested Le Mans, reserving their assault for 1973.

The season started with the Buenos Aires 1000km race with a one-two for the 312 PB. Daytona had been reduced to a six-hour event and here again the 312 PB ran out first.

Further bodywork changes were made for the Monza endurance race; longer tails were fitted with full-width rear deck fenders. Rain fell most of the time, flooding the track, and reduced the winners' speed by as much as 40mph from the previous year (around 146mph). Ickx and Regazzoni beat a Porsche 908/3 with Peterson/Schenken in third place. During the race most of the cars left the track at one time or another and unfortunately Redman/Merzario damaged their car too badly to continue after such an excursion.

Spa was the usual high-speed event without much drama apart from Peterson who found a damp patch on the circuit and crashed. As a change

Left: The 1965 P2 cars were completely new, and one of the first Ferrari racers to discard the traditional wire wheels for cast-magnesium wheels. This was one of the Maranello Concessionaires' 'favored customer' cars.

Right: The Guards Trophy, Brands Hatch in 1965. Mike Parkes in a 375 P2, chassis number '0826,' leads his team-mate up into Druids. The car was converted from a prototype into a Group 7 sportscar.

the Redman/Merzario car crossed the line in first place followed by Ickx/ Regazzoni. Ferrari was no doubt in two minds about commiting a 312 PB for the rugged and arduous Targa Florio but at the last moment sent expert rally driver Munari to partner extrovert Merzario. They won with a margin of 16 seconds from an Alfa Romeo after a hard 492 miles.

The usual three car team went to the Nurburgring and for once they were matched for speed by a Mirage. The result, as on other occasions, was a one/two for the 312 PBs with Peterson/Schenken followed over the line by Redman/Merzario. Regazzoni crashed while being chased by a Mirage.

Driver changes took place at the Osterreichring and there was no 312 PB on the front row. All the cars, including the Ferraris, seemed to suffer from one problem or another but, for all that, the 312 PBs made it a 1-2-3-4 finish.

Watkins Glen wound up the season with a 6-hour race. Record or not, Ferrari made it again with a first and second place thus completing 10 wins in the 10 starts for the championship.

The 625 LM

The 4th Supercortemaggiore 1000km race took place at the Monza circuit on 24 June 1956 and was for sportscars with an upper limit of 2-liters. Three of these cars, the Testa Rossas, were entered for the event and all had Carrozzeria Touring bodywork. The cars were a Ferrari team effort consisting of Vittorio Jano, Alberto Massimino, Andrea Fraschetti, and Luigi Bellantani who had taken over after the departure of Lampredi during the summer of the previous year. The Peter Collins/Mike Hawthorn team won with Fangio/ Castellotti third and Genebien/de Portago 4th. At Le Mans, one month later, the same cars were on hand but had been fitted with 2.5-liter engines which were identical to the 625 formula 1 units. The organizers had insisted that entrants proved 100 cars had been built of the type entered but, of course, Ferrari could not show any such proof and they were entered as prototypes and designated 625 Le Mans. In view of their lack of power — only 225bhp at 6200rpm and their maximum speed down the Mulsanne straight of approximately 144mph against the 156mph of the D-type Jaguars, they came in a creditable third and fourth.

The 330 LMB/330 LM

The World's Sports Car Championship was dropped for 1962 when a new championship for gran turismo cars was instituted. Those responsible for the new rules were in some doubt as to whether the championship would attract sufficient entries and — just as important — enough interest for the motoring press and spectators. In view of this the rules were sufficiently flexible to include the up to 3-liter sportscars and experimental or prototype gran turismo cars of up to 4-liters.

At the Nurburgring and Le Mans 1962 the factory ran a 4-liter car which from the outward appearance could hardly be distinguished from a GTO. In a press release before the Le Mans race Ferrari gave it the designation 330 LM berlinetta and the 4-liter engine was of the type used for the 400 Superamerica gran turismo cars.

At his press conference early the following year (1963) a development of the 330 LMB was shown. The new offering had an engine similar to that of the 1962 car but the chassis was new and the wheelbase had been increased. The car was designated 330 LM and was clothed with beautiful body work which was a combination of the best features of the GTO and the 250 GT berlinetta Lusso. The front was pure GTO with the aggression displayed by that car and the rear had the softer flowing line of the Lusso.

The front mounted V12 unit had a displacement of 3967cc, a single overhead camshaft per bank of cylinders, a single plug for each cylinder, coil ignition and 6 Weber 42 DCN carburetors (for the 1962 Le Mans car and the three 1963 cars) while the 1962 Nurburgring car had 3 Weber 46 DCF3 carburetors. The 4-speed transmission was in unit with the differential. Front suspension was independent with double wishbones and coil spring with a rigid rear axle with semi-elliptic springs.

The 212 E Montagna/Sport 2000

This one-off flat 12 was a development from the 1.5-liter formula 1 car of 1965 but was enlarged to 2-liters in 1967 using one of the Dino 206 S spyder chassis. Originally designated the Sport 2000, its purpose was to compete in the 1968 European Mountain Championship but for one reason or another it

did not run. It reappeared in 1969 using a developed Dino 206S chassis and was then designated 212 Montagna.

The flat 12 boxer engine had been developed by Jacopon and had a displacement of 1990.8cc, double overhead camshafts per bank of cylinders, single plug, coil ignition 4 valves per cylinder, Lucas fuel injection and a compression ratio of 11.0:1. It delivered 320bhp at 11,800rpm. The 5-speed transmission was located behind the mid-mounted engine. Front suspension was independent with double wishbone and coil springs while at the rear there was a single upper arm with a lower wishbone and coil springs.

For the European Mountain Championship, Peter Schett took the wheel and, winning 7 out of the 8 rounds, was unbeatable, collecting new records on the way. The car having already easily won the championship, did not turn up for the final event.

The Dino 166 P and 206 S

Except in the early years when Ferrari reigned supreme, he had shown little interest in formula 2. During 1964 the CS decided on a change of displacement for formula 2 racing to take effect from 1 January 1967. It is probable that Ferrari took a hard look at what the new formula for cars with a capacity of up to 1600cc might do for his commercial prospects world-wide, having noted Porsche's sales with smaller displacement gran turismo cars.

With this in mind Ferrari made a deal with FIAT for them to produce a small engine which, as it turned out, benefitted both parties financially.

At his press conference in December 1964 Ferrari made an oblique reference to the production of a 168 Dino GT with a view to the possibility of

building a 1600cc V8 and said he would give further details during 1965. It was thought that this car would be based on the 1500cc V8 with which John Surtees had won the 1964 World Drivers Championship. Some five months later the factory came up with the Dino 166 P coupe which made its debut at Monza for the 1000km race on 25 April. The 65 degree V6 double overhead camshaft engine placed behind the cockpit was in-line and had a swept volume of 1592cc. Carburation was by 3 Weber twin-choke downdraft 38 DCNs with coil ignition by two Marel distributors. With two plugs per cylinder and a compression ratio of 9.8:1 the power output was around 180bhp at 9000rpm. The 5-speed transmission was in unit with the differential. Suspension was independent all round with double wishbones and coil springs. The chassis was a lightweight multi-tubular framework with riveted-on stress panelling. While Dunlop disk brakes were carried outboard at the front, they were inboard at the rear.

Ferrari unveiled two cars at his press conference in February 1966 – the 330 P3 and the Piero Drogo Carrozzeria Sports Car bodied Dino 206 S.

The 206 S engine had been much modified although it still retained the 65 degree V6 and used the same bore and stroke of the mountain unit. The combustion chamber form had been improved and the compression ratio reduced from 12.8:1 to 10.8:1. A single plug replaced the two plug ignition and the prototype had 3 Weber 40 DCN2 carburetors subsequently replaced by the 42 DCN 2. Fuel injection trials were being carried out. The power output was quoted as 218bhp at 9000rpm. The 5-speed transmission was in unit with the differential. Suspension was independent all round with double wishbone and coil springs. While the car was slightly longer it had the same wheelbase and rear track of the 166/206 P, although the front track had been increased by 12mm to 1360mm.

The coachwork can only be described as a scaled-down version of the 330 P3, being beautifully proportioned with elegant lines. Whilst the overall height was a little greater than that of the 166 P coupe the cockpit area was smoother from the hood line.

Their first appearance was at Monza for the 1000km race which took place in dreadful weather, making the screen wipers quite useless. The first outing was not exactly a success; one works car managed a ninth place and the Maranello Concessionaires entry was placed 13th.

There was every intention of building 50 of this tipo for homologation as a 2-liter Group 4 Sportscar but there was a great deal of industrial unrest in Italy at the time which not only affected production of all cars but also the preparation of the racing and sports racing cars. Also Ferrari, as was his habit, was trying to combine formula 1 racing with sportscar racing and these factors had a detrimental effect all round.

Some 18 206S prototypes were built with varying modifications either made singly or in various combinations; there were one or two plug engines, a choice between carburetors or fuel injection and as a final touch some units had 3 valve heads.

Left: An ex-Maranello Concessionaires Team 330 P2.

Above: The engine from the car on the left. It has six Weber downdraft carbs and twin-plug ignition.

Right: Jacky Ickx's 312 P at the Monza 1000Kms. The 312 P used the Grand Prix car's flat-12 engine in a detuned form, though each bank still had twin cams driving four valves per cylinder. Maximum power output was 440bhp at 10,800rpm, compared with 12,600rpm in the Grand Prix engine at the time.

Competition Berlinettas

V12s front-engined up to 3 liters

Ferrari started racing sportscars shortly after he had formed his own Scuderia in December 1929 but these were not, of course, his cars but either Alfa Romeos owned by wealthy young Italians who raced under the Scuderia banner, or cars which he raced for the Alfa Romeo company.

When he severed his connection with Alfa Romeo in 1938 he formed his own company, Auto-Avio Construzioni, and he still had a number of friends around him, all well versed in automobilism, and more than willing to assist in the building, from FIAT parts, of two sports racing cars for the 1940 Mille Miglia. They were the eight-in-line Vetture 815.

Come the end of the 1939-45 war Ferrari was all ready to restart in the racing game and in the November/December 1946 number of the Italian journal *Inter-Auto* there were details of a Ferrari engine intended for use in competition sportscars and with some tuning for single-seat racing cars. The specification was for a V12 with the included angle between the cylinder blocks set at 60 degrees.

The 166 Spyder Corsa/166 Mille Miglia
The 166 series was introduced in 1948 with a capacity of 1995cc. The Spyder Corsa had cycle type fenders and was used for sports racing but could be used for formula 2 without fenders. Probably 10 of these cars were built before being replaced by a series of spyders with Superleggera bodies by Touring.

There were two groups of these 166 Mille Miglia with somewhere around 30 in the first, built between 1940 until late 1951 mainly with Touring bodies and the second of possibly 12 cars constructed from late 1952 into 1953 were, in the main, spyders with Vignale bodies. However, among the 42 or so all told, there were a dozen closed coupes.

Although all these early V12 Ferraris had a small swept volume they were more than a match for a number of the larger capacity racing cars. In 1948 their main victories were in the Targa Florio (Clemente Biondetti), Mille Miglia (Biondetti) and the Paris 12-hour (Chinetti).

During 1949 there wasn't a sportscar to match the 166 MM, which continued its winning ways from 1948. The Targa Florio was again the preserve of Biondetti and in the Mille Miglia Biondetti and Bonetto posted a one-two while Chinetti and Lord Selsdon won the Le Mans in a 166 barchetta. Chinetti then went on to win the Spa Francorchamps 24-hour event in July.

The 212 Export
There were two models of the 212 introduced in late 1950 – one, the Inter, was for sale as a road version while the Export was for racing. Both models were in production into 1953 with about 110 built with bodies by Touring, Ghia, Vignale, and Pinin Farina, with Vignale having the greatest share.

1951 began well for the 212 Export with Vittorio Marzotto and Piero Taruffi taking first and second places in the Tour of Sicily in April, while, later in the month, Luigi Villoresi won the Coppa Inter-Europa. Although Piero Scotti could only make 3rd place in the Mille Miglia the race was still won by a Ferrari - the 340 America — driven by Villoresi. After this the tipo had a lean time but made a comeback in September when Franco Cornacchia was 2nd in the Targa Florio and Bobbie Baird won the Tourist Trophy in England. Perhaps its greatest success came in November when two 212 Exports were placed first and second in the long distance Carrera Panamericana with Taruffi/Chinetti winning, the second car being handled by Alberto Ascari/Villoresi.

The 250 MM

Based on the 250 Sport this tipo was displayed in chassis form at the Paris Salon in September 1952 and was intended for competition by customers. There were 17 Pinin Farina coupes, 13 Vignale spyders, and 1 Vignale coupe.

The V12 engine had a capacity of 2953cc and followed the almost universal specification of earlier cars except that it had a 4-speed all synchromesh transmission and 3 Weber 36 IF4C carburetors. Power output was 240bhp at 7200rpm. Suspension front and rear was basically similar to the early sportscars. It was not a fast car, having a top speed of 158mph but was extremely handy on any short twisting circuit.

Major competition successes for the tipo were hard to come by as a works car, but in 1953 Villoresi gained a first and Farina a third at the Autodrome Grand Prix at Monza while Paolo Marzotto won the Dolomite Gold Cup at Belluna. Furthermore, in 1954, Trintignant and Piotti were the first over the finish line in the Hyeres 12-hour race. Not altogether surprisingly, as it was built for privateers, its successes in their hands were quite numerous wherever racing was to be found.

The 250 Mille Miglia was a most handsome car, in fact the best looker up to the time it was built and is now one of the most sought after by purists — which means that they command very high prices.

Previous pages: One of the classic 250 GTOs. This one is a 1962 model before the restyle in 1964.

Above left: Inside the 250 MM. The quality of this restoration is plain to see.

Left: Chassis Number 0040 of a 1950 Tipo 166 MM. MM for Mille Miglia.

Above: A 1953 250 MM. Based on the 250 Sport, they are one of the more highly desirable early Ferraris.

Right: Inside a 1948 Tipo 166 Spyder Corsa. Not the most luxurious of interiors, but it wasn't exactly built for long-distance touring.

Left: Three Webers, two coils and 200bhp at 6000rpm. Again, a beautiful example of the restorers' craft.

Below: The 250 Testa Rossa. 'Red Head' by name and nature, this car has a 3-liter V12 power and one of the most beautiful Ferrari bodies ever. The name actually came from the color of the crackle finish engine cam-boxes. This is a 1957 model, one of the first.

The 250 Testa Rossa

For the 1000km race at the Nurburgring on 26 May a new and important prototype sports racing car was entered. It was with this series, the Testa Rossas (a name derived from red crackle finish on the cam covers), that Ferrari pinned his hopes on regaining the Worlds Sports Car Championship for cars up to 3-liter displacement. He had also hoped that some of the production would be bought by privateers for competition, and felt that as the V12 gran turismo cars had been proving successful in races it was logical to develop the unit still further for sports racing.

It was joined for the Le Mans by a second prototype handled by Gendebien/Trintignant which at one stage was lying second until it was retired with a broken piston.

At his annual press conference on 22 November 1957 Enzo Ferrari introduced the 250 Testa Rossa for 1958. The V12 unit had a displacement of 2953cc, a single overhead camshaft per bank of cylinders, one plug per cylinder, coil ignition and 6 Weber 38 DCN carburetors. The 4-speed transmission was in unit with the engine and with a compression ratio of 9.8:1 had a useful power output of 300bhp at 7200rpm. Suspension was independent at the front with double wishbones and coil springs and at the rear was a rigid axle with semi-elliptic springs.

The customer cars had similar specifications but were fitted with an elegant pontoon fender at the front which was introduced on the Le Mans prototype in 1957. This type of front end was not wholly satisfactory as it tended to lift on fast straights and, after a production of 19, was abandoned in July 1958. These customer cars also had left-hand drive.

The works TR58 were entered for the Buenos Aires 1000km in January 1958 coming 1st and 2nd and driven respectively by Phil Hill/Collins and von Trips/Gendebien. The cars were similarly placed at Sebring but Musso replaced von Trips as co-driver for the second place car. Some modifications had been made by the time of the Targa Florio on 11 May. An all-enveloping body had replaced the earlier pontoon fender car, a 4-speed transaxle took care of the transmission and rear suspension was De Dion. This car was entrusted to Gendebien/Musso which led from start to finish with older types third and fourth. A really mixed bag of TRs arrived for the Nurburgring endurance race with old and new body shapes, old and new transmissions. Stirling Moss won in the lone Aston Martin but the TRs occupied 2nd, 3rd, 4th, and 5th places.

Ten Testa Rossas were entered for Le Mans, nine being the V12-engined cars and one 4 in-line 500 TRC. Three of the V12s had the new transmission and De Dion rear axles and one car also had a reversed hood air scoop. Hill and Gendebien won but the other two factory cars retired. Le Mans gave Ferrari his fifth World Sports Car Championship.

During the 1959 season significant changes were made. The wheelbase and bodies were shortened and high full-width windshields were fitted. Over the year both the Colombo and Lampredi-type engine had used hairpin type valve springs but now coil valve springs were used after Ferrari heard of higher reliable rpm to be obtained by the use of coil springs – standard practice in the States. It all seemed to work, as 300bhp was achieved with 8000rpm.

The season opened at Sebring on 21 March when the 1959 250 TRs took 1st and 2nd places, but at the Targa Florio race all the TRs seemed to suffer with rear axle failure and it was Moss who won again in an Aston Martin at the Nurburgring.

Ferrari failed for the second time in the year at Le Mans when three team cars retired with engine troubles. Ferrari's cure was to adopt dry sump lubrication. At this point Ferrari led the Aston Martins by two points in the championship but at Goodwood for the Tourist Trophy Tony Brooks could only finish 3rd so the title went to Aston Martin.

There were further modifications for the 250 TR in 1960. All-round independent suspension for the cars appeared at the annual Le Mans trials and the wheelbase was shortened even further. To comply with the FIA regulations high full width windshields plus wipers (much disliked by all drivers) were fitted. Because of the new dry sump lubrication system and a new 4-speed, all indirect-geared transmission, the engine was placed lower in the chassis. Since all-round independent suspension was used these cars were now designated TRI/60.

1961 saw a complete revision of bodywork for the 250 Testa Rossa when Carlo Chiti replaced Andrea Fraschetti, who was killed while testing way back

in 1957 as design engineer. Chiti had a wind tunnel installed and is probably best known for his early body designs on the mid-engined specialized SP cars. He lowered the nose on the TR61 cars and added the distinctive touch of the twin nostril. The rear deck behind the cockpit was raised and a spoiler added across the width of the Kamm tail to deflect the noxious fumes of the burnt fuel from the exhaust pipes on deceleration.   There were five events counting towards the World Sports Car Championship in 1961. Sebring on 25 March came first with three of the new TR/61s entered. The chassis was a space frame with independent suspension all round and an increased wheelbase. Two of the cars at Sebring had the twin nostril treatment while the third had the older nose-piece. Other cars entered privately were several TR/60s, including the 1960 Le Mans winner, driven by the Rodriguez brothers for NART, some front-engined Dino 246s, several 250 SWBs, a California Spyder and a new 246 SP having its first outing. Phil Hill and Gendebien took the chequered flag with the TRI/61 with a hybrid TRI/61 driven by Mairesse/ Baghetti second, followed by the NART entry. Sharp and Hissom were fourth in a TRI/60.

Ferrari won the Targa Florio with the mid-engined 246 SP but Maserati won for the second year running at the Nurburgring. Ferrari still added 6 points to his score as the Rodriguez brothers placed their TRI/61 second. Third was a 246 SP followed by two 250 GT swb berlinettas.

Not yet totally convinced that mid-engined cars could be trusted he sent Hill and Gendebien and Parkes/Mairesse to Le Mans with TRI/61 cars which came first and second. NART's TRI/61 was present but third place went to the Guichet/Noblet 250 swb.

Although Ferrari had won the championship he sent a 246 SP to contest the Pescara 4-hour on 15 August. He also loaned a TRI/61 to Scuderia Centro Sud for Bandini and Scarlatti to drive. They won.

Its last major event was at Sebring 1962 when the TRI/62 (not an official designation) was entered by Scuderia Republica de Venezia and driven by

Left: The 1952 340 Mexico, one of only three coupes, built for the Carrera Panamericana race across South America. Oddly, they were built with right-hand-drive for circuit work.

Right: Another 340, this time a 340 MM. Built much like the 340 Mexico, the MM was intended for racing and came with 300bhp, five-speed transmission and a multi-plate competition clutch.

Below right: Inside a 375 MM. Unlike its predecessor, the 340 MM, the 375 MM proved quite a success and so tractable that many were converted to road cars.

Bonnier/Bianchi took first place, ending the career of the 250 Testa Rossa and also the career of the front-engined competition cars apart from the gran turismo designs.

V12s front-engined over 3 liters

The 340 America
In the late summer of 1950 Ferrari announced his first big sportscar, the 340 America, and the brochure issued in October gave the details. Apart from the 275S, the 340 America was the first Ferrari, other than the formula 1 cars, to make use of the Lampredi 'long block' engine. The 4101cc unit was similar in specification to the 275 S but the power output was only 220bhp at 6000rpm.

The first tipo was on show at the 1950 Paris Salon. There were probably 25 examples built, including the two 275 S which were brought up to 340 specification. Touring built both barchetta and berlinetta bodies while Vignale built the coupes and spyders. During 1951 the 340 America scored two victories with Villoresi winning the important Mille Miglia race and Olivera the Portuguese Grand Prix at Porto on 17 June. A number of these sports racing cars crossed to the States where their owners won a number of races.

The 340 Mexico
In 1952 Ferrari built four of these cars, three coupes and one spyder built by Vignale for the 3rd Carrera Panamericana. The spyder was never entered for the race as it was bought by Bill Spear of the States and competed successfully in that country.

Specification was similar to that of the 275S and the 340 America but used DCF3 carburetors and had a longer wheelbase than the 340 America. They had a rating of 280bhp at 6600rpm.

This tipo had scant success and the race for which they were prepared was won by Bracco in a 250 MM. The 340 Mexico berlinettas (coupes) of Luigi Villoresi/Franco Cornacchia and Ascari/Giuseppe Scotuzzi did not finish the race.

The 340 MM
The tipo was a more powerful version of the 340 Mexico with 300bhp available. There was a slight difference in specification using Weber DCF instead of DCF3 carburetors. The wheelbase was shortened but the front track was extended.

It was Villoresi who first brought success to the 340 series when he won the Tour of Sicily in April with a 340 MM and later in the month, on the 26th, Gianni Marzotto won the Mille Miglia with Tom Cole in fourth place and Giulio Cabianca ninth.

With these two failed tipos, although they could not be matched for sheer speed, Ferrari had some thinking to do before going back to the design board. While he might have improved the chassis what was really required was probably more development of existing components. How often, over the years, have we seen a tipo shelved before it has been fully developed?

The 375 MM and 375 Plus
Le Mans 1953 saw the initial appearance of the 375 MM driven by Ascari/ Villoresi. The berlinetta was bodied by Pinin Farina on a long wheelbase and had the looks of a stretched 250 MM. It was said by the pit staff that the engine was a development of the car prepared for the 1952 Indianapolis 500. The car set the lap record but retired when plagued by clutch problems. Also at Le Mans were two 340 MM berlinettas and these were brought up to 375 specification. There was also a Vignale spyder 375 MM and the four cars represented the works for 1953.

The V12 had a displacement of 4494cc. Magneto ignition replaced coil and the 3 Webers were type IF/4C or 42 DCZ carburetors. A 4-speed transmission was in unit with the engine. There were two versions – the works and customer cars and the works car had a power output of 320bhp at 7000rpm.

1954 saw a more powerful Ferrari, the 375 Plus. The compression ratio was increased slightly to 9.2:1 and three Weber 46 DCF3 twin choke carburetors were fitted. Power rating showed a minimum increase over the 375 MM from 320 to 344bhp but the mid-range power and flexibility of the engine had been improved. The displacement was now 4.9-liters and the

4-speed all synchromesh transmission was in unit with the differential, the rear axle being a De Dion type located by parallel trailing arms.

The 1954 race record of the 375 Plus was adequate but it did win two important events – Le Mans in June with Gonzales and Trintignant driving and in November Umberto Maglioli won the Carrera Panamericana.

The actual number of 340 MMs built is difficult to assess and the nearest count is between 12 and 18 with most bodies built by Pinin Farina either as berlinettas or spyders. A total of only four 375 Plus were built, all spyders, by Pinin Farina.

The 290 MM

A new Ferrari V12 powered the 290 MM and the engineering team now led by Vittorio Jano developed the best features from the Colombo and Lampredi engines and also used a number of components from the earlier cars. A displacement of 3490cc, twin ignition with 24 plugs and 4 distributors, 3 Weber 40 DCF carburetors and a compression ratio of 9.1:1 gave an output of 230bhp at 7300rpm. A 4-speed transmission was in unit with the differential. Front suspension was double wishbones and coil springs while at the rear was a De Dion tube and transverse springs. Spyder bodies built by Scaglietti to a Pinin Farina design were similar to those of the 860 Monza.

For the important Mille Miglia the works entered five teams. The race was held in appalling weather on 29 April. Fangio and Castellotti each had the new 290 MM, Collins and Musso an 860 Monza apiece while Gendebien drove a Scaglietti lightweight 250 GT berlinetta. The performance by the team was really impressive as was the finishing order – Castellotti, Collins, Musso, Fangio, and Gendebien in the first five places.

The 1000km Sports Car Grand Prix of Sweden run on the Kristianstad circuit hosted the final round of the championship and it was the decider for 1956. Ferrari fielded three 290 MMs. During the race Manson (not down to drive but acting as relief for Collins), had an oil line break spewing oil on the track and, spinning on the lubricant, shot off the circuit into a wheatfield. Collins (in another car) and Phil Hill were behind, hit the oil and also found themselves in the field but regained the circuit. There was much swapping of cars/drivers but Trintignant and Phil Hill brought the V12 home first and Ferrari, taking five of the first six places, made sure of the championship.

The 315 Sport and 335 Sport

Only two were built and both were entered for the 1957 12-hour Sebring race. The cars showed a good turn of speed but suffered various mechanical maladies and could only muster a 6th and 7th place.

Drivers for the Mille Miglia in May were Collins/Klemantaski, de Portago/Ed Nelson and Piero Taruffi (solo). Von Trips, also solo, had a 315 Sport and Gendebien/Wascher a very potent GT berlinetta with a new body style.

Collins went out with rear axle failure before Brescia and the unfortunate de Portago had a front tire blow-out 25 miles from the finish, killing himself, his co-driver, and 10 spectators. Taruffi at the age of 51 and desperate to win, at the thirteenth attempt won at an average of 94.8mph. Von Trips could have passed Taruffi with his faster car but held back and followed him home with the incredibly fast GT berlinetta, third at an average of 93.6mph.

Due to the de Portago tragedy two of the 335s were impounded for inspection so only one was present at the Nurburgring for the 1000km on 26 May. Tony Brooks in an Aston Martin DBR1/300 won.

For Le Mans Hawthorn/Musso shared a 335 Sport but retired with loss of oil pressure after setting a new lap record of 126mph. The 315 Sport managed fifth place driven by Stuart Lewis-Evans/Severi.

The 335 Sports were handled by Hawthorn/Musso and Phil Hill/Collins for the Swedish Grand Prix on 11 August but could only make 2nd and 3rd respectively behind the winning Maserati 400S.

Two 335 Sports and two 250 Testa Rossas contested the 3rd Venezuela Grand Prix. All the Ferraris were look-alike but the 4-liter cars had a small air scoop on the engine lid. The main opposition came from the Maseratis but they were left in disarray – literally – with crashed and burnt out cars strewn around the circuit! The Ferraris made it a 1, 2, 3, 4 and once more took the Championship.

V6 front-engined

The Dino 206S

It is said that the Dino sportscars came as a great surprise to all. On 7 April 1958, at the BARC Easter Monday meeting at Goodwood, Ferrari unloaded the 2-liter V6 front-engined Dino. Collins was there to drive the car for the Sussex Trophy race and to the surprise of all he placed the little Dino behind Stirling Moss's 3.7-liter Aston Martin DBR2 but ahead of Duncan Hamilton's 3.5-liter D-type Jaguar. The car was designated 206S. The 65 degree V6 unit had a displacement of 1983cc. Twin overhead camshafts provided the drive

for two Marelli distributors with ignition by two plugs per cylinder. There were 3 Weber twin-throat 42 DCN carburetors and, with a compression ratio of 9.8:1, the power output was given as between 220 and 225bhp at 8500rpm. These cars had no transaxle and the 4-speed transmission was in unit with the engine. The car appeared for the 40 lap 2-liter event at the Naples Grand Prix on 27 April but was retired with clutch problems after Musso had set the fastest lap.

The Dino 196 S

Ferrari had been discussing his twin overhead camshaft V6 engines with a well-known motoring journalist saying that the twin camshaft layout was too expensive. So it was not really surprising when the next sports Dino appeared with a single cam layout. In fact the V of the 6-cylinder engine now had an included angle of 60 degrees and the car was being tested late in 1958.

The engine resembled half of a V12 Testa Rossa unit but with some modification. The capacity was 1983cc and apart from a single camshaft per bank each cylinder had only one plug. With 3 Weber 42 DCN carburetors and a compression ratio of 9.8:1 it had an output of 195/200bhp at 7800rpm. The 4-speed transmission was in unit with the engine. Only two cars were built, but it does appear that by building this Dino Ferrari had it in mind to have a small run of gran turismo cars based on the general specification. The bodywork was handsome, the design being by Pinin Farina and executed by Fantuzzi.

Race-wise the 196 S was a failure. It appeared at Monza for the Coppa Sant' Ambroeus and in the 43rd Targa Florio it retired with transmission troubles. Giulio Cabianca and Giorgio Scarlatti were the drivers and they also shared the car for the Nurburgring 1000km on 7 June. On lap ten the engine blew up with either a holed piston or a dropped valve.

On 5 September the car contested the 24th RAC Tourist Trophy race at Goodwood but Scarlatti and Scarfiotti failed to finish. At the season's end, during the Nassau festivities, Ricardo Rodriguez placed the 196 S second in an all-Ferrari race.

Previous pages: A 1953 375 MM. A bore and stroke of 84×68mm gave it 4522cc and with a compression ratio of 9:1, this car pushed out 340bhp.

Above: The 1966 206S Dino. With its 65-degree, twin-overhead camshaft, 1987cc engine, the 206S was a scaled-down version of the 330 P3.

Right: The 206S Dino may have lived in the shadow of the P3, but it still gave 218bhp at 9000rpm.

Left: The 500 Mondial Series 2 made its debut at the Bolzano-Mendola hillclimb in 1955. The front suspension was modified from the Series 1 car by replacing the transverse leaf spring with coils.

Right: The 500 Mondial Series 2 had the 1985cc engine from the Series 1 car but power was increased from 160bhp to 170bhp and carburetion was upgraded.

Below right: The 750 Monza, introduced in 1954 at the track that bears the same name. The engine was based on the previous Tipo 555 4-cylinder unit, but featured many unusual design features.

The Dino 246 S

For 1960 Ferrari had an enlarged engined Dino, the 246 S, with a displacement of 2417cc (bore/stroke 85 × 71mm) and still with single cams for the V6 unit. Full information on the engine is lacking but it was reputed to be rated at 248bhp at 7500rpm. As with all sports/sports racing cars for 1960 the 246 S had to comply with the governing body's ruling for full width high windshields so much disliked by the drivers. Like the 196 S the new car failed to make its mark on the racing scene, not winning a single major event.

One car was sent to Buenos Aires for the 1000km race. It lasted 39 laps before the ignition caused problems. At Sebring the Rodriguez brothers had to drop out when the clutch gave trouble. It did look as if the 246 S would come good at the 44th Targa Florio for in the hands of Phil Hill/von Trips it ran a very good second to Bonnier's Porsche.

So ended the careers of the four Dino sportscars but it was hardly surprising that they were failures as the works could not have expected to carry out much in the way of development on them. Their hands must have been full looking after the grand prix cars, preparing and developing the V12 Testa Rossas (after all Ferrari was much involved with the Sports Car Championship), and, since the 250 GT berlinettas were showing such promise in the important gran turismo events the works had to service and repair these customer competition cars. The enterprise seemed costly at the time but Ferrari benefitted when the mid-engined V6 SP cars took to the circuits.

In-line-fours

Ferrari's practice from the earliest days was to design and build engines which could be used, with modifications, for grand prix and sports/sports racing cars and also for gran turismo automobiles. All of this kept down the overall cost of development work and components and at the same time allowed engines to be switched for whatever purpose they were required. When, in 1951, Lampredi was given the task of designing the 2-liter 4-cylinder engine for formula 2 events and the 2.5-liter unit for the future formula 1 (which would restart in 1954), it was natural that the units would find their way into sportscars.

The 500 Mondial

The 2-liter formula 2 engine which had been so successful in 1952-1953 was the basis for the 1954 500 Mondial sportscar which was for both works and customer competition. The first Mondial engine was installed in a conventional Ferrari chassis, probably that of a 250 MM. There were two series, the second appearing in 1955.

The original 4-cylinder unit had a displacement of 1985cc with twin overhead camshafts, two plugs per cylinder, magneto ignition, and 2 Weber 40 DCOA/3 carburetors. With a 9.2:1 compression ratio the power was rated at 160bhp at 7000rpm. A few changes were made for the second series, the power was increased to 170bhp, 2 Weber 45 DCOA/3 carburetors were fitted, and a 5-speed transmission installed. Probably 30 cars were built with the major portion having Scaglietti spyder bodies and a few spyders from Pinin Farina. It is believed that the first Scaglietti body for a Mondial was designed by Dino Ferrari.

The race record in 1953 was most encouraging with a 1st in its class and 2nd overall in the Casablanca 12-hour event on 20 December. At Agadir on 27 February it won its class with François Picard at the wheel and later at Dakar it was again successful in its class and came 2nd overall. Entered for the Mille Miglia on 1 May the 500 Mondial turned in its best performance being placed 2nd overall by Vittorio Marzotto.

The 750/860 Monza

During the winter 1953/54 work started on a new four-cylinder engine derived from the Tipo 555 Grand Prix unit – this was the 750 Monza. As with most Lampredi designs the cylinder head and block assembly, crankcase and sump were aluminum alloy castings with cast-iron cylinder liners screwed into the head to eliminate compression leaks. Displacement was 2992cc and 2 Weber 58 DCOA/3 carburetors supplied the fuel. With a compression ratio of 8.6:1 the power was rated at 260bhp at 6000rpm. A 5-speed transmission was in unit with the differential. The spyder bodies were designed by Dino and built by Scaglietti and it is estimated that about 29 were built.

The competition history of the 750 Monza is not well recorded, which is

strange since so many were built, but it seems certain that on its initial appearance at the Gran Premio Supercortemaggiore run over the Monza circuit on 27 June 1954, Mike Hawthorn took the chequered flag.

In 1955 a larger version of the Monza contested the Tourist Trophy race on 17 September with Castellotti/Taruffi at the wheel but it was never in contention. The car was designated 860 Monza with a capacity of 3431cc. With a compression ratio of 8.6:1 the rating was 310bhp at 6200rpm. The main specifications followed those of the 750 Monza but it had a 4-speed transmission in unit with the differential. Probably around 10-12 were built.

The 860 Monza didn't do too badly in 1956 starting with the Sebring race in March when Fangio and Castellotti beat Musso and Harry Schell to the line taking 1st and 2nd places. This was followed on 8 April as Peter Collins won the Tour of Sicily in a 1955 model and then took second place in the Mille Miglia with Musso third in another 860 Monza while Castellotti won the event in a 290 MM.

500 Testa Rossa and 500 TRC

Lampredi, who had been with Ferrari from 1947 except for a period of a few months, left in the summer of 1955 and went to work for FIAT in Torino. Jano, who had joined Ferrari when the Lancia Grand Prix cars and their equipment had been handed over to the Scuderia, was now part of the new engineering team which included Alberto Massimino, Luigi Bellantani, and Andrea Fraschetti. They came up with a new 2-liter sports racing car — the 500 Testa Rossa. On 28 April 1956 Ferrari showed his new offering at the New York show and on 24 June three of the cars were entered for the 1000km Supercortemaggiore race at Monza, which was for 2-liter cars. The cars were bodied by Carrozzeria Touring, the first time Ferrari had used Touring since the 340 MM.

The design was similar to the Monza and Mondial which Scaglietti had built but they had exaggerated wheel arch cut-outs. The three 500 TRs came

first, second, and fourth respectively. At Le Mans, one month later, the TRs were equipped with 2.5-liter engines (probably those used in the 625 F1 cars) and Ferrari had to enter them as prototypes and designated them 625 LM. Although the Jaguars and Aston Martins had the legs of the 625 LMs the Trintignant/Gendebien car finished third.

Ferrari announced a new 500 Testa Rossa late in 1956 which was built to comply with the FIA's 1957 Appendix C regulations. The car was called, quite logically, the 500 TRC. Scaglietti was commissioned to build the bodies which were lower by three inches than those of the 500 TR.

The specifications (apart from the 625 LM) for both tipos were similar; 4 in line engines with a displacement of 1984cc, double overhead camshafts, 2 plugs per cylinder, coil ignition, and 2 Weber 40 DCO/3 carburetors. Compression ratio was 8.5:1 and power output 180bhp at 7000rpm. The 4-speed transmission was in unit with the engine. Front suspension had double wishbones and coil spring with a rigid axle at the rear with coil springs.

The competition Gran Turismo Berlinettas

From his early days as a constructor Ferrari had not only raced sportscars but also berlinettas in the same classes since such cars were basically sportscars with a roof. This could, of course, be said of some of the gran turismo berlinettas which came along at a later date and which were built specifically for long distance endurance events. The term berlinetta, in Italian, can be translated as 'little sedan' or, more usually, as coupe.

In very general terms the road gran turismo berlinetta was a heavier car, with more interior comfort and refinement than its counterpart, used almost solely for racing. This latter model usually had a lighter aluminum body with perspex for the windows and windshields, the interior stripped so as to be quite stark and containing only equipment essential for racing.

By 1955 sportscar racing had reached the stage where the cars were no

Left: The 250 GT LWB (long-wheelbase) Berlinetta was powered by the V12 Colombo-designed engine. The power output varied with its compression ratio, but was around 250bhp.

Right: From 1951 right through to 1961, Ferrari dominated the Tour de France, an event which took in some six-circuit races, two hill-climbs and a drag race. The 250 GT LWB Berlinetta was unofficially re-named Tour de France after the win in 1956.

more than two-seater grand prix cars. It took the tragic accident at Le Mans in that year before the FIA changed the rules to establish new classes for gran turismo cars.

The 250 GT LWB Berlinetta

Ferrari, as was so often the case, was prepared, for he had been in production with a 250 GT berlinetta since 1954 with a long wheelbase chassis. The familiar 60-degree V12 Colombo-designed engine powered these cars which had a displacement of 2953cc with a single overhead camshaft, single plug, and 3 Weber 36 DCL 3 or 36 DCX 3 carburetors. Transmission was via a single dry-plate clutch and 4-speed all synchromesh transmission in unit with the engine. Front suspension was independent with double wishbones and coil springs with a live rear axle and semi-elliptic springing. With a compression ratio which varied between 8.8 and 9.5:1 the output was from 230 to 280bhp at 7000rpm.

Ferrari had Pinin Farina design some lightweight bodies executed by Scaglietti which, with variations, became the customer competition car between 1956 and 1959. The original design was based on the 375 Mille Miglia competition berlinetta but had tail fins added to the rear of the rear fenders and louvers behind the doors. The fins were subsequently removed. The grille was fussy in design and the headlights were exposed but slightly recessed in the front wings. Over the years the lights were recessed further into the front fenders and covered with molded perspex being faired into the fenders.

The 250 GT long wheelbase berlinetta was named (but not by the factory) the Tour de France subsequent to De Portago's win in that event in 1956. The Tour de France was a tough event which featured six races on major circuits, two hill-climbs, and a drag race, apart from the long distance timed rally. Ferrari had first won the Tour as long ago as 1951, was second in 1952 and 1953 and then had a sequence of wins from 1956 to 1961. In 1960 Ferraris took the first three places and filled the first four in 1961!

Left, right and below: Some 200mm shorter than its short-wheelbase counterpart, the 250 GT SWB Berlinetta Lusso was the last of the 250 series and remains one of the most graceful Ferrari shapes. There were two versions, road and race, the road version coming with steel bodywork and much more luxury (Lusso) in the cockpit.

The 250 GT SWB Berlinetta

The Paris Salon of 1959 saw the introduction of the 250 GT short wheelbase berlinetta, a development of the long wheelbase model (the different wheelbases being 2400mm and 2600mm). There were two versions — the road cars and the competition cars, both having the same engine specifications as the earlier 250 GT berlinetta but with varying equipment.

The competition 250 GT swb had lighter bodywork and obviously stark interiors while the customer road cars were built with steel coachwork, a more luxurious interior, and softer suspension. The lines of the 250 GT swb followed fairly faithfully those of the 'interim' berlinetta but the quarter lights had been eliminated and the rear from the back of the cockpit roof had a more rakish angle as the overall length had been truncated. It was a handsome and purposeful-looking car. While the customer road cars had steel bodies the doors, hood and trunk lid were aluminum.

Due to changes in body style and wheelbase the FIA did not homologate the 250 GT swb berlinetta as gran turismo cars until shortly before the 1960 Le Mans event. Before this it had to be entered in sportscar classes. As already noted the race was a Ferrari 'walk over' taking all placings up to 7th except for 3rd. The first 250 swb berlinetta home was 4th overall and 1st in the GT class. The 5th, 6th and 7th places also went to berlinettas.

While Stirling Moss had had a contract for one race (in the fifties) from Maranello he did not run as he blew his engine in practice which was not a popular thing to do as far as Ferrari was concerned! However, in 1960, privateer Rob Walker had bought a 250 swb berlinetta which he entered in the 25th Tourist Trophy on 20 August. Moss drove and he not only won the race but a week later with the same car won again at Brands Hatch. The short wheelbase car continued to win its races in 1960 and 1961 with an occasional lapse against such opposition as the Jaguar XK-E and the Aston Martin GT.

All in all this was a tipo which combined ultra good looks with superb performances whether on the circuits, in rallies, hill-climbing and even as a static display in concours, and it will certainly live in the minds of all those fortunate enough to have seen it in competition.

Apart from the Tour de France the long wheelbase berlinettas notched up a number of memorable wins in its class in a variety of races from the Tour of Sicily to the Mille Miglia and was almost capable of holding its own against more powerful machinery including other Ferrari tipos. The 250 GT long wheelbase berlinetta is one of a number of Ferraris which will always be sought after by the knowledgeable Ferrarist and will therefore command a high price in the market place. While the 250 GT short wheelbase berlinetta which followed is even more sought after it didn't have such a distinguished racing history, winning fewer races than its predecessor.

Before the 250 GT swb berlinetta an 'interim' long wheelbase berlinetta model was produced which displayed rather softer body lines indicating that a change of coachwork style was about to take place. It was a handsome car but only 7 were built before the short wheelbase car came on the scene.

The 250 GTO

In 1962 the FIA changed the rules for the Sports Car Championship and substituted two new categories: one for gran turismo cars and the other for prototypes. To qualify for the former at least 100 models were to have been built during a single year's production. Ferrari had been working on a new model for the new category, the 250 GTO, and being the man he was he persuaded the FIA that the new car was but a development of his 250 GT swb berlinetta. After all, where would the new GT class be without Ferrari participation? So the new tipo was homologated and the 'O' tacked on to the GT meant in Italian 'omologazione.' It was this new tipo designed and built by the factory engineering department which won the GT championship three years in succession (1962, 1963, and 1964).

The 250 GTO was a strikingly handsome-looking car by Scaglietti with the long low nose close to the ground and the lamps faired into the front fenders. Overall it was lower to the ground and sleeker than its predecessor, the 250 GT swb. The car was shown to the press in February 1962 when it wore a nose to tail stripe of red, white, and green (the Italian colors).

The 60 degree V12 engine with a displacement of 2953cc was based on the Testa Rossa unit and throughout its production used a dry-sump lubrication system. It also used 6 Weber 36 DCN carburetors. Drive was via a single

Above left: The fearsome 250 GTO, one of only 40 units. Such is the legend surrounding this car that almost every one is fully documented and researched. And prices for the few examples that are not 'copies' are reaching well over $1,500,000. Stories of people having sold them years ago for next to nothing are almost as common as people who knew the Beatles!

Below left: Another example of this most impressive of Ferraris. There were actually four different types of 250 GTO — the most common is the 3-liter Series 1, then the 4-liter Series 1, the 3-liter Series 2 and just one 3-liter car with Le Mans Berlinetta bodywork. This car was only named a GTO because the factory chassis records included it as such.

dry-plate clutch with an all synchromesh 5-speed transmission in unit with the engine. Suspension was similar to the short wheelbase tipo, although it has been suggested that coil springs should be used at the rear replacing the semi-elliptics, but it was thought such a change might cause delay in obtaining homologation but coils were used around the tubular shock absorbers.

Sebring in March 1962 was its first outing when Phil Hill and Gendebien were 2nd overall and 1st in the GT class. For the race there was a small change to the bodywork as a spoiler had been 'tacked' on to the rear. All subsequent cars received the same treatment until the spoiler became an integral part of the rear end.

On 6 May the GTO was again 1st in class at the Targa Florio and 4th overall. At the Nurburgring on 27 May two cars were entered but one failed to restart after a pit stop (it had been leading the GT class) and the other crashed on the sixth lap. For the event the factory had also entered a prototype GTO of 4-liters (a 400 Superamerica engine with dry sump lubrication) which Parkes and Willy Mairesse drove to 2nd overall.

Le Mans, two weeks after the Nurburgring, saw the Pierre Noblet/Jean Guichet GTO taking first in the GT Class and 2nd overall while two other GTOs finished 3rd and 6th overall.

The GTO continued to win race after race during 1962 culminating in the Paris 1000km run over the Monthlery track when they took 1st, 2nd, 4th, and 5th places, the winning car driven by the Rodriguez brothers Ricardo and Pedro.

At his annual press conference in December 1962 – for the 1963 season – Ferrari had no new cars on show and intimated that only a few more GTOs would be built for, as he said, it was only the top drivers who could handle such fast cars. Production was limited to 39 GTOs including the three 4-liter cars over a three year period.

While the new car for 1963 was the 250 P which made an auspicious start at Sebring on 23 March, posting a one-two, the GTO continued to make its presence felt in all the important events including the eighth win by a Ferrari in the Tour de France! As in 1962 the last big event in the year's calendar was won by a GTO in the GT class in the Nassau Tourist Trophy and was also 2nd overall.

The 1964 version of the GTO was basically the same as the 1963 model but visually was very different but still extremely handsome and known as the Series II car. A wide air inlet at the front replaced the smaller elliptical opening with the additional air inlets on either side. The windshield was sharply raked and virtually a wraparound. The cockpit area was set well back from the long hood and the rear of the driver's compartment had sail panels which gave the rear deck the appearance of a sugar scoop. Three cars were built as originals and from the earlier production four chassis were re-bodied to 1964 styling.

The Series II GTO got off to a good start at the 1964 Daytona 2000km with Phil Hill/Pedro Rodriguez crossing the line first and followed home in 2nd and 3rd places by similar cars driven by Piper/Bianchi and Hansgen/Grossman respectively. This was followed up by a GT class win at Sebring on 21 March when Piper/Rodriguez/Gammino shared a 64 GTO.

The GTOs had plenty of competition in the GT class during the season with the Shelby Cobras, E-type Jaguars, and Porsches to contend with, and at the Nurburgring 1000km the Ford Motor Company made its competition debut.

The season progressed with the GTOs still making their mark. The final event counting towards the Manufacturers' Championship was the Tour de France and once more Ferrari gained the honors with Bianchi/Berger first and Guichet/de Bourbon y Parma in 2nd place, both in 1962/63 GTOs. Ferrari won the championship with the Shelby Cobras in second place.

Ferrari had still hoped to get the 250 LM homologated for 1965 but the FIA were adamant over their ruling so he decided not to contest the GT category that year. In fact it was suggested that the GTO would be the last front-engined Ferrari to contest the GT classes but it so happened that competition versions of the 275 GTB and 365 GTB/4 were built.

The 275 GTB/C

Two new models were on view at the Paris Salon in October 1964 – the 275 GTB (berlinetta) and 275 GTS (spyder) with coach design by Pinin Farina and built by Scaglietti. There was probably no intention to build a competition model as both were passenger cars and the first Ferraris to have independent suspension all round.

Eleven cars were built in 1966 for GT racing and featured some of the

changes made in that year for the production models such as a longer nose (which gave greater elegance to the overall shape). The body was aluminum alloy and with other weight saving, some 150kg was knocked-off the normal passenger model. It had a Lusso-type hood blister which covered the six Weber carburetors, and the nose was certainly similar in some respects to both the GTO and the 330 LMB.

The factory entered a car for the Nurburgring 1000km driven by Baghetti/Biscaldi which did not show up too well, although in practice Bandini had been much faster than the GTO.

The 365 GTB/4
Once more at the Paris Salon Ferrari was to spring another surprise, although rumors of a new super car had been bandied about for some time. The date was October 1968 and the car the 365 GTB/4 with a Lampredibased 60 degree V12 front-engine. It was probably the most exotic passenger car built by the factory and without doubt the fastest road car in the world with genuine top speed of 174mph. Pinin Farina had been the designer and Scaglietti, as usual, built the coachwork.

For a gran turismo car it was heavy, being about 1808kg (3615lb), but Luigi Chinetti, boss of NART, prepared a car for the 1971 Le Mans 24-hour race to be driven by Coco Chinetti and Bob Grossman. They posted 5th overall and it was thought they were 1st in the GT class but for some unaccountable reason a Porsche 911 was given as the winner.

This promising debut decided the factory into producing a few berlinettas which were designated 365 GTB/4A competizione. Weight had to be pared and this was reduced by nearly 200kg. Wide wheels and tires were necessary and the compression ratio was raised to 10.0:1 which resulted in a power increase from 352bhp/7500rpm to 402bhp at 8300rpm. Theoretically the top speed might be expected to be 200mph but whether this was ever achieved is doubtful.

The 4390cc four overhead camshaft engine had six Weber 40 DCN 20 carburetors mounted on the inside of the Vee. Two Marelli distributors sparked the single plug per cylinder and the 5-speed transmission was in unit with the differential.

The Daytona, as the car was generally known, had one big fault — brakes which had a tendency to fade all too rapidly and this was certainly a disadvantage for any model intended for racing. The brakes were Dunlop ventilated all round, and the brake fluid would also boil. Chinetti added a dual master cylinder (minus servo assistance) and also better coil air ducting.

While the factory was never to enter a Daytona in a race they were more than happy to assist in the preparation of the cars used by their concessionaires, various equipes, and privateers. In general the Daytona acquitted itself well as apart from its speed it was certainly a most reliable car.

The 308 GTB
Although the 250 LM could be called the first mid-engined car built by the factory for gran turismo class racing it was not until 1966 that homologation was bestowed on the tipo by the FIA. But it was really too late and in any case

Left: Successor to the 250 GT Lusso, this 275 GTB coupe came with more power than the GTS Spyder version, usually the 280bhp compared with the 260bhp on the GTS.

Above: The 365 GTB 4 Daytona coupe, another on the Ferrari enthusiast's 'most wanted' list. At 4.4 liters, rated at 352bhp, it used a rear-mounted transaxle and is capable of 180mph. The body was by Pininfarina.

Right: Privateers, Biscaldi and Baghetti, campaigning their GTB at the 1965 ADAC 1000Kms at the Nurburgring.

Previous pages: The 275 GTB/4 debuted at the Paris Salon in October 1966 and was fitted with the dohc version of the Tipo 226 V12.

Left: The 308 GTB appeared in 1975 and was the first Ferrari to feature all-fiberglass bodywork, produced at the Scaglietti factory.

Below left: The 365 GT4/BB was the first flat-12, mid-mounted engined Berlinetta to come from Ferrari.

Right: The 308 GT4 2+2 was designed by Bertone. Scaglietti built them and the engine was the 255bhp, 4-cam, 3-liter, V8.

the 250 LM could not, in truth, be considered a GT car being in reality a two-seat racing car with a roof.

The 308 GTB is also mid-engined with a 3-liter V8 engine set transversely in the chassis. The 308 series included the 308 GT4 2 + 2 and the Mondial 8 2 + 2. The fact remains that all the cars built in the series were passenger vehicles with no pretensions to being converted to gran turismo racing. A number have been raced by amateurs and semi-professionals but only at club level.

Apart from rebodying the chassis of the 308 GTB to the normal Group 5 configuration, the main modifications were to the mechanics. To give a higher volumetric efficiency and some other advantages 4 instead of 2 valves per cylinder head were fitted with the added boost of turbocharging. Using twin Garrett blowers, the Carma FF Biturbo 3-liter V8 had an outstanding power output of between 840 and 860bhp, 'trimmed' for race purposes to 750bhp!

The race record is of some interest since it is the only 308 to have been raced seriously. At Daytona for the 24-hour event it set the fastest lap at 127.65mph before retiring with electrical and cooling problems on lap 4. Mugello saw the car in second place but an argument with a Lancia put it back a place where it continued until the engine gave up after 20 laps racing. Practice for the Monza event put the 308 on pole – the car had been timed down the straight at over 200mph. Unfortunately a turbo broke on the warm-up lap which put it out of the race. There was another retirement in the Silverstone race with a variety of problems. For the Nurburgring event the car was sidelined as it had been too badly damaged during practice to be repaired in time. Pole position was again achieved at Enna but it was 'flaming' on the third lap and retired once more. Kyalami was its last appearance in 1981 (it did not run in 1982) when after running for 2 hours of the 9-hour race the engine really blew up!

Perhaps with some help or advice from Maranello some reliability might have been built into the car. In any case Maranello must have watched its progress with some considerable interest and perhaps they are wise in not placing their faith in a turbo passenger car.

The 365 GT4/BB

The 365 GT4/BB was the first flat-12 mid-mounted engined berlinetta to be introduced by the works. Although displayed at the 1971 Turin show it didn't go into production until 1973. There can be no doubt that it was a fast pas-

senger car built for comfort but not racing. Despite this there is always someone around willing to convert almost any berlinetta Ferrari into a race car.

One of the first was that old campaigner Luigi Chinetti and his NART outfit. However, since there is little evidence that anyone else wanted to race the model it may be assumed that the NART car was the only one ever to be raced and it is doubtful whether the factory was ever interested! The car was lightened by removing all unnecessary equipment and the body modified to accommodate the wide Goodyear tires. No doubt some work was carried out on the engine as the power output was alleged to be between 400 and 420bhp whereas the road version's output was 380bhp. Never competitive, it retired after covering one lap for the 1975 Daytona race but it did finish 6th at Sebring. At Road Atlanta mechanical failure put it out during practice and the engine caught fire at Lime Rock.

It was not raced in 1976 but appeared at Le Mans in 1977 where it finished 16th after a two-hour delay in the pits. Daytona 1978 was probably its last race when electrical problems set in so that it crossed the line in 22nd place.

The 512 BB

The 512 BB was introduced at the 1976 Paris Salon as a replacement for the 365 GT4/BB. Visually there appeared to be little difference but on close inspection the new car had a 'chin' spoiler under the front grille and NACA ducts low down on the body sides and just in front of the rear fenders.

The flat-12 boxer engine was given an extra 552cc over the 365 GT4/BB model bringing the displacement up to 4942cc. But it was rated at only 360bhp – a power drop of 20bhp although the maximum speed was increased slightly to an estimated 188mph.

While the previous road berlinetta boxer received scant attention from the factory as regards racing, the new 5-liter model was to have some encouragement. Ferrari had abandoned sports and gran turismo racing some years previously concentrating on formula 1 (a sign of Fiat influence perhaps?). Maybe Fiat were seeing the folly of this policy as Ferrari sales over the years had relied to a great extent on racing successes and not just from the formula 1 cars. Whatever the reason the factory gave support, even if it was limited, to a number of concessionaires and privateers wishing to race the 512 BB.

For 1979 the works stepped up development showing a greater interest in the car's competitiveness. Work on the body shells was carried out in Pinin

Left: The 512 BBi took the flat-12 engined Ferrari idea to new heights. Very fast, yet very comfortable.

Below: A massive 380bhp at 7200rpm, and a torque figure of 318lb ft at 3900rpm made for one of the most rapid road-going cars Ferrari ever produced.

Right: As if to prove just how fast they were, this 512 BB was seen at Le Mans where LM versions competed for a few years in private (usually French) hands.

Below right: One of the last 512 BBi cars before the limited edition, 'new' GTO versions, a 1982.

Farina's wind-tunnel and the cars, now known as the Silhouette Boxers, were 16 inches longer (10 inches added to the nose and 6 inches to the tail). The headlamps were behind fairings within the front spoiler with the roof line continuing via a near horizontal sloping rear window right down to the tail which had an aerofoil across the rear deck supported by two vertical fins. The mechanics were virtually unchanged but with Lucas fuel injection the power output was 475bhp at 7200rpm. The transmission, always a weak link, had stronger competition-type straight cut pinions. Water and oil cooling systems were enlarged and the transmission had its own oil radiator. The rear suspension was modified with two spring/damper units on each side with an American Indy type pneumatic jack mounted alongside. The cars were tested at both Fiorano and Fiat's Nardo tracks.

In preparation for the Le Mans race a great deal of testing took place, the Michelin tires being the main target. Four cars contested the race – two from Ch. Pozzi, one from NART, and one from Ecurie Francorchamps. The Ferraris ran in the IMSA class (International Motor Sport Association), a cross between Group 4 and Group 5 as defined by the FISA. This meant that their main rivals were the turbocharged Porsche 935s.

There was some justification that the 512 BBs would do reasonably well at Le Mans after their initial outing at Daytona but the NART and Ch. Pozzi entries failed to finish. The two Pozzi cars crashed when trying to pass slower cars, one was lying 6th after 19 hours. The only finisher ran out 12th, having had a number of problems on the way.

Early 1980 saw two new 512 BBs on test at Monza; these had modified bodywork and mechanics. The body between the front and rear wheel arches below door level was extended downwards giving an impression of ground effects skirts. The main research on the engine was directed towards fuel consumption where a 10% reduction was achieved without reducing the power output.

Le Mans saw six cars entered (three 1979 models and three 1980 versions) – Ch. Pozzi took three cars (2 new and one older model) – NART a 1980 version which did not start as the engine threw a rod in practice – one Italian run under the Scuderia Supercar Bellancauto banner and the British ex-Ecurie Francorchamps car owned by Steve O'Rourke.

Wet weather during the early part of the race affected the electrics of the Ferraris necessitating numerous pit stops. Only two of the cars finished after various traumas – a Pozzi entry finishing 10th overall and 3rd in the IMSA category and the British entry lasting the 24 hours was 23rd overall and 8th in the IMSA class.

The 512 BBs did rather better in 1981 with two privately entered cars taking 1st and 3rd places in the IMSA class and finishing 5th and 9th overall. The NART and British entered cars were retired and Bellancauto had bad luck for the second year running, this time with 'disarranged' mechanics.

Although getting older five 512 BBs were due to contest Le Mans in 1982 but a private French entry failed to materialize. The familiar NART and Ch. Pozzi entries were present but perhaps the most striking car was the privately entered Ron and Patti Spangler Prancing Horse Farm 512 BB in Ferrari red with black and gold stripes and gold decals. Lasting the 24 hours it was placed 6th overall and 3rd in Group IGTX.

For a car which was built as a 'supercar' for road use and not designed for racing, all credit must go to the concessionaires and private owners who saw the possibilities of using it for endurance racing and to the works for giving some support even if it was limited.

Up to the present no turbocharged 512 BB has been seen on the circuits although one was entered for the 1977 Le Mans event. An unnamed Hong

Left: Built almost entirely on race lines, the 1984 GTO featured sparse, business-like interior trim.

Below: The GTO was developed with the aid of large deposits from eager purchasers. Numbers were limited to an initial 200 cars. Built from steel and Kevlar using race-car construction technology, the resemblance to the 308 was only skin deep.

Right: A GTO engine. Based on the 4-valve V8, it produced 400bhp, a top speed of 189mph and 0-60mph in under 5 seconds.

Kong enthusiast asked Louis Chateau to prepare such a car. Chateau had experience with the turbocharged Porsches but decided that as the 512 BB's lubrication system did not lend itself to conversion for racing purposes, so the project was abandoned. Before the abandonment, however, a body had been built which was somewhat reminiscent of the Porsche 917. The car was given the 'code' name 512 Turbo GTP but had nothing to do with the factory.

288 GTO

In 1983 Ferrari announced what was then the fastest road car they had ever built. Selling for around $100,000, initially (although the cars have always changed hands for more than that), and destined to be built in a limited run of 200 vehicles, the GTO was, many observers concluded, designed to re-establish the on-the-road driving credentials Porsche had stolen in sportscar racing during Maranello's absence.

Indeed there were many people who concluded that the resurrection of the most evocative Ferrari badge of all meant that the new GTO was, like its

illustrious forerunner, designed for the racetrack. The truth is that almost any Ferrari is equally at home on road or track, and the fact that the road cars are developed on the same 1.86 miles of Fiorano test track as the formula 1 cars may well have something to do with it. However there was more reason to think it with this car. In 1983 Ferrari announced their production schedule of 200 road cars, plus some 30 or 40 of what they called 'evolution' models – which were intended to be for racing use. And if the market exists, Ferrari said, they may build a further 100 road cars. *If the market exists!*

As soon as the car was announced people were sending money as deposits from all over the world, and this car established something of a precedent for low-volume car makers. The success of the GTO proved that merely by announcing a car would be built, a manufacturer could collect a substantial sum in deposits – not enough to finance it, but enough to make it worthwhile. Aston Martin openly said that it was this very reasoning that prompted their launch for the new Zagato.

The GTO, when it emerged, looked very similar to the 308, although only the doors were common parts. Also Pinin Farina had to adapt what was then accepted as a classic shape to a car which was different in just about every vital dimension. Bigger in most ways, the GTO is lighter than the 308 by 250lb and a whole 800lb less than the 512.

The secret is in a formula 1-derived steel and composite body and chassis, which uses Kevlar for the hood and the bulkhead between driver and engine, and fiberglass for the body panels. Much design and development work was conducted under the influence of Ferrari's formula 1 designer Dr Harvey Postlethwaite, who applied racetrack experience directly to the GTO and confirmed that in turn the GTO would serve as a testbed for the production process of advanced materials.

The chassis is a tubular spaceframe which makes extensive use of high-strength steel and includes an integral rollover cage. Tubular side structures extend behind the cockpit to carry the engine and here the twin-turbo V8 is mounted lengthways rather than sideways as in the 308. The suspension is traditional Ferrari, with unequal length wishbones and Koni dampers.

The engine was not new either. It was based on the quattrovalve production V8, and delivered 400hp at 7000rpm. That was enough to give the GTO a top speed of 189mph and accelerate it from 0-62mph (0-100kph) in just 4.9, very busy, seconds. Perhaps a more convincing demonstration of the turbo V8's power is the 0-125mph time of a mere 15.2 seconds.

The capacity is just right for FIA Group B competition rules for the 4-liter class, thanks to the 1.4 multiplier which is applied to turbo engines. Giving a maximum of 11.8 lb/in sq, the two Japanese IHI turbos give the GTO an FIA racing capacity of 3997cc. The use of two turbos to overcome lag draws heavily on Ferrari formula 1 experience. The two small units use lightweight alloys in their installation and deliver their boost through two Behr heat exchangers and then a Weber-Marelli fuel injection system. An engine management computer controls this and the action of the electronic breakerless ignition.

Despite this, and despite the advent of Porsche's much-admired 959, the GTO was a no-compromise race car with no hint of modern microchip-controlled miracles like ABS braking, variable valve timing or 4-wheel-drive. 'We did not want 4-wheel-drive for this car' said Ferrari, also dismissing ABS braking for the same reason: neither systems have the flexibility needed for racetrack success. 'What is important,' said Ferrari, 'is that the GTO's brakes are efficient.'

They are ventilated discs front and rear with dual-pot calipers giving good initial bite and progressive stopping power thereafter. Ferrari believed that the driver should be free to use and modulate their action as necessary, claiming that in certain racing situations, wheel lock is a desirable quality unobtainable with ABS.

The fenderwells were made large enough to enclose the 12-inch racing tires permitted for racing, but the road cars were supplied with 8-inch rubber at the front and 10-inch wide rear tires.

Inside, the GTO offered almost as much nostalgia as its name suggested. Trimmed entirely in black, the seats have small metal eyelets which provide useful ventilation and which were very popular in the sixties. There is less room than in the 308, despite the extra inches outside; the honeycomb bulkhead bows outwards into the passenger compartment, restricting elbow room and limiting seat travel. The facia and instruments are the same as the 308, and the steering wheel abbreviates the edges of the dials in just the same way.

The F40

After the GTO succeeded the 308 there were some far-flung rumors concerning an IMSA GTP racer from Maranello. Occasional artists' impressions of a short, squat car with a tall rear spoiler were followed by spy photos of a car which was definitely a Ferrari and definitely seemed to bear out the rumor. And then the car eventually went public. Prototype sportscar racing is clearly the place you would expect to find the F40, yet it remains one of the fastest *production* cars ever made. It was built, said Ferrari, in order to celebrate the fortieth anniversary of the Ferrari badge. And unlike the short production run of the GTO, Ferrari envisaged that eventually a total of up to 1,000 F40s would be built.

Incredibly, even for Maranello, this is a car capable of some 200mph, with a 0-60mph time of less than 4 seconds – a potential which by normal standards belongs on the racetrack. And there were many fans who hoped that the announcement of the F40 in the summer of 1987 would signal a return to Le Mans – especially interesting as traditional rivals from Porsche began a discreet withdrawal in the face of opposition from Jaguar.

The possibility seemed all the more likely since the F40 is crammed with the lessons and hardware of the formula 1 circuits. The powerplant, up from 2855cc to 2936cc, is basically that of the GTO, though basic is hardly an appropriate word for a twin-turbo V8 that produces 478hp at 7000rpm. Everything about the car is to racetrack quality, even the fuel cells, which are already homologated and need only a quick-fill cap to make it ready for competition.

The car is basic in other respects, though, and creature comfort is given the scant regard with which race drivers are more than familiar. People parting with sums beyond $200,000 might find the uncarpeted aluminum floor, sliding window, and plastic pull-cord instead of a doorhandle slightly upsetting. In fact there is little or no trim at all – the dashboard is the same as for Ferrari competition cars and leaves the composite from which it is formed bare and uncovered. The only concession is a perforated vinyl roof lining;

even the pedals are plain drilled metal without even black rubber capping. 'Instrumentation,' said Ferrari, 'has been kept to the bare minimum.'

The seats are hard-formed racing chairs, ventilation is poor at best. And there can be no escape from the noise of that V8 engine which sits inches behind driver and passenger. The message is very clear – this is not an executive toy or even an expensive sports tourer. This is a race car with enough legality built in so that you can drive it on the road.

The message is underlined by a typical Ferrari six-finger gate, a heavyweight clutch, and a tacho redlined at 7750 rpm. Despite all that, it is as tractable from low rpm as the GTO, on which its engine is based – the two turbos come into action quite low down but produce explosive amounts of power from 4500rpm upwards. Yet the engine was designed to be docile, and pull from low rpm quite easily, and with the turbo-boosted torque curve satisfactorily thick in the lower reaches of the rev scale there is no doubt this has been achieved.

Nevertheless, the engine is packed with competition-derived tricks, with eight butterflies on the inlet manifold, operated as one, hollow exhaust valves, silver/cadmium con rod bushes, oil-cooled piston crowns, and water-cooled turbochargers. The engine management system takes turbo boost pressure into account when calculating fuel quantities for each of the 16 injectors (there are two per cylinder), controls ignition (through four coils), and controls the turbo wastegate valve; rather than the 'domestic' management system, it is derived directly from the more complex formula 1 'black box'.

The results, measured by Ferrari at Fiorano, show the F40 to have a top speed of 201.3mph and a 0-125mph time of just 12 seconds.

The penalties for this kind of performance are large in road-going terms. The ride is harsh and stiff, and not eased by the massive tires. Pirelli P Zeros are fitted all round, 245/40 VR17 on 8-inch rims at the front and enormous 335/35 VR17 on 13-inch rims at the back. The steering is heavy by everyday standards, perfectly balanced for race-track work.

The suspension is adjustable through three ride heights, one for parking,

one for everyday driving, and a third for high-speed work. The brakes – large 330mm Group C racing discs – are cast iron over aluminum to reduce unsprung weight. All the pipes and unions are to formula 1 quality. 'Obviously,' said Ferrari, 'the system does not envisage the use of a servo brake.'

Outside, the F40 provides continual reminders that it ought to be a Group C race car, that it ought to be competing at Daytona or Le Mans rather than traveling the main roads of Europe or the USA. Its styling is brutal compared to its stablemates, its necessary venting and louvers interrupting its business-like wedge and dominating rear spoiler. Its massive need for the intake of cooling air is probably one of the main reasons its snub, blunt body has a Cd figure which reaches down only to 0.34; Ferrari are often very coy about quoting aerodynamic numbers on production cars, and it's easy to see why even though they are leading exponents of wind-tunnel science.

When compact saloons all over Europe can achieve Cd0.28, why are Ferrari and Pininfarina so far behind? There's more to airflow management than Cd numbers, and as the F40 proves conclusively, Cd is by no means the only arbiter of a successful design – nor of ultimate performance. In any case, 0.34 was the target figure; it was achieved within a design brief which required Pininfarina to create a design which would 'arouse the desire to own a race car which could be used on the road.' To this end the appearance of the car was also intended to be evocative of functional racing designs, and little concession is made to styling; there's no sign of the window-dressing which conceals the Testarossa air intakes, and there are ducts and inlets all over the bodywork.

The body is formed in composites, a lengthy and expensive process (the rear deck lid takes three days), and is bonded to a tubular frame with a structural adhesive. This is the first real production usage of techniques which derive directly from the state-of-the-art formula 1 bodies.

The aim of the anniversary project, said Ferrari, was 'to return to a concept in vogue in the fifties and sixties when customers with their everyday Ferraris dominated the race tracks throughout the world.'

Left: The F40 production line. Demand for this car has reached such proportions that some F40s have been sold many times even before they are delivered.

Above: A 512 BBi engine. It comprised four Weber carbs, twin belt-driven overhead cams and a quoted 380bhp.

Right: The F40 interior lacks creature comforts, but it is built for speed and that's what it does best. Note the woven Kevlar construction of the cockpit floor.

The 328 GTB

In 1985 the 328 GTB made its debut at Frankfurt. It was similar in looks to the 308, but bigger in every respect. Wheelbase had risen by 12 inches and was now 8ft 8in. Designed by Pinin Farina, it was built by Ferrari, and quite frankly looked identical. There didn't seem to be anywhere, apart from a modest front overhang, which could account for its extra inches. The styling of the 308 had changed in small ways during its life, especially with the advent of the qv version. The body had changed from fiberglass to steel with the advent of the 308 GTS. Now small aerodynamic changes were introduced, particularly affecting air intake size and shape. And the 328 shared the Testarossa-style rear lights.

The suspension, remaining traditional Ferrari, was redesigned to improve roadholding by including anti-dive geometry and negative scrub radius or zero offset at the front, and some similar alterations at the rear. And at the same time the provision was made for optional ABS braking. Inside there was a new dashboard, redesigned to improve visibility, access, and equipment levels.

Under the hood was the new generation of the V8 engine, modified to raise capacity up to 3185cc and featured four valves per cylinder. The extra valves had featured on the 308 GT Quattrovalvole as well, in late 1982, but the new engine had still more to offer.

Part of the story was in new piston design, with a pronounced squish effect for better combustion, and a change from Digiplex electronic ignition to the more sophisticated Microplex type. There were new camshaft profiles, and different spark plugs to take advantage of the better breathing. All that meant a power increase, from the 240hp of the 308 to 270hp, both figures attained at 7000rpm. There was a 17 per cent increase in torque as well – as would be expected with the extra valves. That gave the 328 a quoted top speed of 161mph, and a 0-60mph time of around 6 seconds.

Previous pages: The F40 in all its glory. The chances of seeing one of these on the road, where they belong, is very slight indeed.

Above: Detail of tail-light of the 328 GTB. Overshadowed in almost every respect by the awesome F40, the 328 GTB can still hold its head up in serious supercar company.

Left: The 328 GTB Quattrovalvole engine with its advanced electronics and 307bhp. Acceleration to 60mph is a startling 6 seconds, with a top speed of 161mph.

Right: Since its introduction in 1985 at the Frankfurt Show, the 328 GTB has never looked back. Demand for the car has never been higher, and its eventual replacement is eagerly awaited.

Formula 1 Racing Cars

Enzo Ferrari was in the racing game with cars bearing his name for forty years and during that time his cars notched up a total of 84 world championship races. Not a spectacular number perhaps but nonetheless a respectable total.

In 1958 a constructors' or manufacturers' championship was instituted and Ferrari only won the title on six occasions – 1961, 1964, 1975, 1976, 1977, and 1979. He was also top constructor in 1952 and 1953 and, taking into account the Lancia-Ferrari D50, in 1956 as well, although none of these years are to be found in the records. To round off his achievements he was runner-up to the title in 1958, 1959, 1966, 1970, 1974 and 1978 and before the championship, in 1951. Statistics may be boring but the measure of the man's talents can best be set out simply by figures.

Apart from his constructors' titles, seven of his drivers have won nine World Drivers' Championships (started in 1950). Alberto Ascari won the title in 1952 and 1953 driving the almost unbeatable 500 F2 and Juan Fangio in his only year as a contract Ferrari driver was successful in the 1956 Ferrari-Lancia D50. Mike Hawthorn just pipped Stirling Moss for the championship in 1958 driving the 246 and 256 Dinos and the only American to win the title was Phil Hill driving the 156 F1. In 1964 John Surtees (seven times World Motorcycle champion) won the championship with the 158 F1 but it was another nine years before another Ferrari driver, Niki Lauda, was the title holder, winning in 1975 with the flat-12 312B and 312T and in 1977 with the 312 T2. South African Jody Scheckter who started off the 1979 season in the 312 T3 and had the use of the 312 T4 later in the year was the last man to become World Driver Champion in a Ferrari.

So much for the overall picture of how Ferrari survived over the many years of his involvement in motor racing and it is to his credit that he kept going even when nothing seemed to go right. He did on occasions make it known that he wanted no more to do with the sport but such pronouncements have been made by many sportsmen in the past in the heat of the moment. Ferrari's main protagonists have been the Italian national press (when winning ways are not forthcoming they scream abuse) and the governing body of the sport. Ferrari always held a strong if not always a fair hand when dealing with the authorities, for any grid at a Grand Prix without at least one red car would not be a Grand Prix in the true sense.

The 125 F1

While Ferrari had a competent group of technicians around him after World War II he was lacking a designer to enable him to fulfill his early ambition. Gioacchini Colombo was an obvious choice and a man whom Ferrari had known since 1924 when he joined the Alfa Romeo concern as a draftsman. Colombo had progressed at the Portobello firm under Vittorio Jano but had become disenchanted with his position towards the end of the thirties when Jano had been forced out and replaced by an obnoxious Spaniard, Wilfredo Ricart. So the transition to help Ferrari when asked was not difficult.

Work on a 60 degree V12 engine started in 1946 and although a sports racing car, the 125 C, was the first to appear, in May 1947, the 1.5-liter supercharged racing car did not make its debut until September 1948 at the Italian Grand Prix on the road circuit at Valentine Park, Turin.

The first tipo 125 F1 grand prix cars were not exactly successful on the circuits but this could be said of many 'first-off' designed cars. Ferrari was lucky in having a great development engineer in his team – Luigi Bazzi – whose job it was to solve the problems as they arose.

The detachable cylinder-heads, block, and crankcase were cast in aluminum. Wet cylinder liners were shrunk in and the heads held them in compression against the block. Each bank of cylinders had a single overhead camshaft and the exhaust and inlet valve per cylinder were actuated by rocker arms.

A single Weber 40 DO3C carburetor was situated in the V of the engine and the Roots-type supercharger was mounted at the front. With a compression ratio of 6.5:1 the power developed was only 225bhp which was well below that of its main rival the Alfa Romeo 158 with 310bhp at 7500rpm. The only way to compensate for the lack of power was to use a light tubular chassis. This was a ladder-type structure of oval section tubing with two main longitudinal members, a box-section cross-member at the front and, to support the aluminum body panels, tubular cross members and a welded framework. It had a short wheelbase which was a contributory factor to instability at high speed. Front suspension was by double wishbones of unequal length and a transverse leaf spring while the rear suspension incorporated torsion bars. Damping was by Houdaille vane-type shockabsorbers and the hydraulic brakes had finned alloy drums.

Previous pages: Chris Amon at Spa for the Belgian Grand Prix in 1967 where he managed third in the V12.

Left: The final Grand Prix of 1954, the Spanish at Barcelona. Mike Hawthorn won it in the Tipo 552 Squalo.

Above right: The 1949 Tipo 125 F1 complete with two-stage supercharger and 6.5:1 compression ratio.

Right: The 1948 Gran Premio d'Italia. Raymond Sommer is in the rain at Turin's Valentino Park.

Three cars were entered for the 225-mile Italian Grand Prix which was run in appallingly wet weather with Farina, Sommer, and Bira as drivers.

Farina, when running fourth, lost control on the wet road and rammed some straw bales damaging the radiator, while Bira retired on lap 66 with transmission failure. Sommer took third place after a race-long duel with Villoresi's Maserati.

The Ferraris did no better at the Autodrome Grand Prix held over the Monza circuit but there was some consolation at the minor Circuit of Garda race when Farina won easily from Sterzi's Spyder Corse 2-liter car with Villoresi's Maserati third. The Spanish Grand Prix held over the street circuit at Pedralbes was another flop. Farina and Bira went out with transmission problems and José Pola blew his motor.

At the end of the season the works retained one car and built two new cars. The main changes were twin overhead camshafts per bank of cylinders, twin-stage supercharging, a longer wheelbase, and a rear leaf spring over the rear axle. Power was increased to 300bhp at 7500rpm. The revised models were not available until late in the season for the Italian Grand Prix (also the

European Grand Prix in 1949) at Monza on 11 September which Alberto Ascari won for Alfa at 105.04mph.

Without those main rivals – the Alfa Romeos – to contest the events for 1949 the 125 F1 had a fair season with five first places and two seconds with two top drivers – Alberto Ascari and Luigi Villoresi, who had good backup from amateur Peter Whitehead who had some support from Maranello.

The basic Colombo engine design was multi-purpose and this was evident during the early years when a number of sportscars were produced such as the tipo 166 Spyder Corse. The unit was also put to good use for formula libra and formula 2 racing cars. By increasing the displacement to 1995cc Ferrari had his tipo 166 formula libra car with a single Weber 40 DORC carburetor and single stage supercharger with an output of 310bhp at 7000rpm. The formula 2 car had the same capacity, no supercharger, three Weber 32 DCF carburetors, and a power output of 155bhp (raised to 160bhp in 1950/51) at 7000rpm. These cars were highly successful in single-seat form, winning many races during 1949/50 and 1951, but the day of Ferrari's smaller capacity engines was nearly over with the departure of Colombo back to Alfa

Below left: The 4.5-liter Tipo 375 F1 debuted at Monza. It was left with no serious competition when Alfa Romeo pulled out of racing at the end of 1951.

Right: For the 1952 season, the new World Championship was based on formula 2. The Tipo 500 F2 with its 1980cc twin overhead-cam engine and 180bhp, won 14 world championship races in a row in 1952-3.

Below: The view from the driver's seat, as seen by drivers like Ascari, Taruffi and Villoresi.

Romeo and his replacement by his number two, Aurelio Lampredi. Ferrari was not a man to continue along a set line when he could foresee advantages to be gained by following a new one although, at times, he needed convincing that new ideas would be to his benefit. At this time only a small amount of cash could have been coming his way with the sale of surplus racing and sports racing cars, for he had hardly touched on the commercial market for passenger cars, so an all-out effort would have to be made to gain world-wide recognition. This, he deduced, would be by advertising his wares on the racing circuits as other constructors had done in the twenties and thirties.

Ferrari had obviously seen the benefit to be gained by enlarging the capacity of Colombo's original design and discarding the extra boost obtained by supercharging. Supercharging meant thirsty engines which in turn meant more pit stops for fuel and to overcome the time wasted for refueling meant a greater speed advantage over any rivals. He could also see that a large capacity unit would provide him with an engine with a long development life.

Lampredi, who had been advocating the larger engine, was an empirical engineer. He had a 'feel' for automobile engineering which stood him well during the years he was with Ferrari and having had the benefit of Colombo's training was more than ready to tackle any new project. His job was threefold – to design a 4.5-liter V12 unblown unit to beat the new Alfa Romeo 159,

to prepare a 2.5-liter four-in-line cylinder car for the 1954 season when new regulations for formula 1 racing would come into effect and finally to design a 2-liter four-in-line cylinder unit for formula 2 racing. The latter car was in part speculation but Ferrari had a suspicion that for 1952/53 the grand prix competition would be for formula 2 cars and not formula 1. As usual he guessed absolutely right!

The 375 F1

Although Lampredi followed the basic design of Colombo's 60 degree V12 engine there were distinct differences. Known as the 'long block' unit, overall length was 42 inches (Colombo's was 37 inches).

The Italian Grand Prix at Monza on 3 September saw the race debut of the 4.5-liter 375 F1. Cars were provided for Ascari and Serafini. Ascari's engine failed so he then shared Serafini's and they managed a creditable 2nd after a race distance of 312 miles. Two of the new cars contested the Penya Rhin Grand Prix over the Pedralbes street circuit on 29 October. Ascari won and was followed home by Serafini and in third place Taruffi brought his 4.1-liter 340 F1.

Alfa Romeo had stayed at home during 1950 but came back to do battle with the 4.5-liter Ferraris in 1951. The 375 Fl had had a busy season racing in minor and major events and up to the time of the Spanish Grand Prix, run as usual at Pedralbes. On 28 October it was a 'toss-up' as to whether Maranello or Portobello would take the season's honors. There was not a manufacturers' title to be won as this was not instituted until 1958 but there was prestige to be won. Perhaps the odds were in favor of the Ferraris as they had scored a 1, 2, 3 the previous year over the same circuit, but for 1951 the race distance had been increased from 194 to 275 miles.

Ascari was on pole with Fangio (Alfa Romeo) alongside but tire problems beset the Ferraris. Fangio won and Froilan Gonzales snatched second place from Farina with Ascari 4th, one lap down on the winner. So Ferrari lost the final battle with Alfa Romeo and Ascari had to be content with second place in the drivers' championship.

Having squeezed the last ounce of power from the Alfa's 159 engine and as the Italian Government had not been forthcoming with an expected subsidy to keep them afloat the Portobello firm had to say goodbye to top-line motor racing for some 20 years or so.

With no competitors around, the 375 F1 cars were now obsolete as regards formula racing and buyers had to be found to get rid of them.

The 500 F2

As expected, the powers that be decided that the championship for 1952 and 1953 should be carried by the formula 2 cars. Ferrari was ready with his well-tested Tipo 500 F2 – a model that was almost unbeatable and bringing the factory a great deal of prestige.

Left: Chassis Number 500/0210/F2. Beautifully restored, yet no longer allowed to turn its wire wheels in anger.

Right: All the cars prepared for the 1956 French Grand Prix at Rheims had the new 'bigger bore/shorter stroke' V8. Peter Collins took the win that year with Castellotti second.

Below right: The British Grand Prix at Silverstone in 1956. Peter Collins pulled in with no oil pressure, De Portago pulled in to give Collins his car, and Castellotti pulled in after crashing his. De Portago tried to re-enter the race in Castellotti's car but was black-flagged after two laps!

Ferrari unveiled the 500 F2 in 1951. The four-in-line cylinder engine had a displacement of 1980cc with twin overhead camshafts, two valves, two plugs, and two Marelli magnetos. The 1951 car had two Weber 50 DCO carburetors but these were replaced in 1952 with four Weber 45 DOEs, and with a compression ratio of 12.8:1 the power output was 180bhp at 7500rpm.

In 1951 Ascari and Villoresi drove the new car in the Modena Grand Prix and dominated practice and the race although Villoresi had to retire at half-distance with engine trouble. Ascari won easily and set a new lap record at 75.53mph.

During 1952/53 the 500 F2 won 14 world championship races in a row and in 33 starts was beaten on only three occasions. Alberto Ascari became World Driver Champion in both years and Ferrari was top constructor.

The 625 F1

Ferrari had planned the new four-in-line 2.5-liter engine as far back as 1951 when the prototype unit for the 625 F1 was placed in the new 500 F2 chassis he was testing. The car was entered in the Bari Grand Prix for Taruffi to drive against heavier metal which included the 4.5-liter V12 375 F1s and the Alfa Romeo 159s. It finished in third place. Its next appearance was at the Valentino Grand Prix, Turin, in April 1952, when Taruffi finished second to Villoresi's 4.5-liter car. And in 1953, in three outings, it was first, second, and third at Buenos Aires and with two cars entered for the Rouen Grand Prix was first and second. In a short sprint at Silverstone, over 50 miles, Hawthorn retired with an overheated engine.

While for many years now formula 1 cars have run on what is virtually pump fuel it is interesting to recall that the fuel mixture used by the 2.5-liter engine was 40 per cent methyl alcohol, 30 per cent benzole, and 30 per cent 100-octane fuel with 1 per cent castor oil added.

Ferrari not only had the 625 F1 (the original 2.5-liter-engined car) for the new 1954 formula but was, in 1953, developing the 553 F1 car, also for the new formula. This tipo was called the 'Squalo' since its bulbous appearance was somewhat shark-like. An entirely new car, it was first tested at the Italian Grand Prix at Monza in 1953. The tipo was a further development of the original Lampredi four-cylinder unit similar in many respects to the 625 F1. Weber designed a special twin-choke carburetor for the tipo, giving it two type 58 DCOAFs. Power output with a 12.0:1 compression ratio was initially 250bhp at 7500rpm from 2497cc. The 4-speed transmission driven via the multi-plate clutch was in unit with the rear axle. Final drive incorporated a ZF limited slip differential and fuel was carried in side-mounted pannier tanks, which were part of the bodywork, and a small tank in the tail.

The 553 F1 and 555 F1

The 553 F1 was supposed to be an improvement on the 625 F1 but proved itself unreliable and for the time being the factory had to rely on the slower yet dependable 625 which chalked up eight wins in 1954 in a variety of races. A great deal of interchanging of parts between the 625s and 553s gave no improvements and the Mercedes-Benz W196 with their 8-cylinder engine and streamlined bodywork had little difficulty in overcoming the ills which beset the Ferrari team.

For 1955, changes were made to both the 625 and 553, the former now designated 625 A and the latter the 555 Supersqualo. Success, however, was not forthcoming and the only win was in the European Grand Prix held at Monaco in May when Maurice Trintignant drove a 625 A with a 555 engine.

The Lancia-Ferraris

The Lancia D50 was showing some promise in 1955 until the company's dire financial position put paid to any further development work and stopped its competition life. Ferrari was getting nowhere with unreliable and out-classed cars and he had nothing coming along until fortune smiled on him from an unexpected quarter. Arguments over the fate of the Lancia D50s resulted in all the cars, their equipment, chief technicians and designer of the D50, Vittorio Jano, transferring to Maranello.

The D50 chassis was a multi-tubular spaceframe with the engine being used as an upper connecting member. Panniers on outriggers held the fuel and were located between the front and rear wheels with an additional small fuel tank in the tail.

The 90 degree V8 engine had a displacement of 2488cc, twin camshafts per bank of cylinders, two valves, two plugs, and twin magnetos. Four Solex 40 P11 carburetors fed the fuel and with a compression ratio of 11.9:1 the power output was 250bhp at 8100rpm. Wherever possible, without weakening any part, Jano had drilled holes and the bodywork was aluminum to keep the weight down.

Under the prancing horse insignia the D50s were entered for the Italian Grand Prix over the Monza road-cum-track circuit. Ferrari was contracted to run on Englebert tires which were not only unsuitable for the Lancias but also for the Ferraris over such a circuit. The D50s were withdrawn but the Ferraris ran with Castellotti making 3rd place.

Overwintering at Maranello was an unwieldy collection of cars – outdated 625s, unmanageable and unreliable 555 Supersqualos, and four Lancia D50s with suspect handling qualities. And in the meantime Ferrari had Juan Manuel Fangio, World Driver Champion, under contract.

Fangio had a modified car for the 1956 Argentine Grand Prix with work carried out on the suspension, and the outrigged panniers had been mated with sheet metal to the main bodywork. He blew the engine during practice and though he started the race with the car had further mechanical problems so switched to Musso's car which had had only minor modifications. He won at 79.38mph and went on to collect first place in the Buenos Aires City Grand Prix at 83.09mph.

Fangio had quite a reasonable season but owed his 1956 Drivers' Championship to Peter Collins who unselfishly gave up his car to Fangio who went on to win the European Grand Prix at Monza on 2 September. Fangio's car had had problems but Castellotti coaxed it into 8th place. Further modifications were carried out during the winter to the engine, attention was paid to the suspension and the cars were now designated Ferrari-Lancia 801 and had a power output of 275bhp at 8200rpm.

1957 was not a successful season for the Scuderia, winning some minor events but only taking some placings in the races which counted. However, during the 1956 season Jano had been working on the first of the Dino V6 cars for formula 2 racing. Its first race was the Naples Grand Prix on 28 April

where it was entered with two Ferrari-Lancia 801s with all the latest modifications for Collins and Hawthorn. The Dino 156 F2 (as the new car was designated) was in the hands of Musso who had a good race placing the car third behind the two larger capacity 801s.

The Ferrari-Lancias had had their day and perhaps Ferrari was not sorry as the cars had not been designed but only developed by his engineering team. Now the factory could get on, after the hiccup, with designing its own cars once more. After all a Ferrari is a Ferrari and not a Lancia!

The 156 F2, 246 F1, 256 F1 and 296 M1

All the V6 cars and some of the V8s, including one gran turismo (the 308 GT4 2 + 2 bore the prefix Dino after Ferrari's son for he was mainly responsible for suggesting this configuration).

The first V6 produced by the works was the 156 F2 which Musso drove in the Naples Grand Prix in 1957 where it was placed third. The engine was quite new with the V at an angle of 65 degrees and with the two banks of three cylinders staggered with the left bank slightly ahead of the right bank. The four overhead camshafts, fuel, oil, and water pumps were chain driven from the front of the crankshaft. Three twin-choke Weber 42 DCN carburetors were located in the engine V and protruding through the hood were covered by a metal cowl with an air intake. There were two plugs per cylinder sparked by twin magnetos originally driven from the front of the inlet camshafts. Transmission was via a dry multi-plate clutch and 4-speed transmission in unit with the final drive. Dry sump lubrication was employed. Chassis was a semi-space frame with front suspension of double wishbones of unequal length and coil springs while at the rear the de Dion tube was behind the transmission with a transverse leaf spring above the final drive unit. Twin radius arms were used at the rear and damping all round was with Houdaille vane-type shock absorbers.

Besides the outing at Naples the car was used in practice by all the drivers at Monaco but was not raced. However, Maurice Trintignant drove the 156 F2 in the Coups de Vitesse which preceded the Reims Grand Prix on 14 July. After a race-long duel with two Cooper-Climaxes (both finally flew their motors) Trintignant scored its first victory.

For 1958 the 156 F2 had a true spaceframe and appeared twice being posted 2nd by Peter Collins at Rheims and 5th at the Nurburgring (in the formula 2 race) by Phil Hill. 1959 produced a 2nd place at Siracusa only. For 1960 the 156 F2 was similar in specification to the formula 1 cars with independent rear suspension (unequal length wishbones and coil springs and the engine angled with the propshaft across the cockpit floor). A 5-speed transmission was installed in unit with a redesigned final drive. Two fuel tanks

Left: One of the 1968/1969 formula 2 Tasman Series cars: an ex-Derek Bell car.

Below left: The Tasman F2 cars used the 2.5-liter V6 Dino engine complete with fuel injection.

Bottom left: Derek Bell took this car to many of the Tasman Series races, including a second at the Australian Grand Prix behind fellow Ferrari driver, Chris Amon.

Right: Monaco in 1959. Jean Behra in the formula 1 246 Dino before his motor exploded on the 25th lap.

Below right: Hawthorn at the British Grand Prix in 1957. The car is a Lancia-Ferrari 801.

were located on either side of the cockpit forming the sides of the body. The first race was at Siracusa which von Trips won after Moss's Porsche had retired but on 24 July at Solituderennen, von Trips had a rear-engined tipo which he took to a narrow win by 3.6 seconds from Hans Herrmann's Porsche. The same car and driver won the formula 2 category in the Italian Grand Prix at Monza.

The final event in which the formula 2 cars participated was at Modena on 2 October. Richie Ginther had the front-engined car and took 2nd place while von Trips had to be content with a third. This was the last formula 1 or 2 race in which a front-engined Ferrari took part.

Ferrari had obviously decided that if the formula 2 cars had proved satisfactory he would go on to build 2.5-liters V6 units for 1958. Also for 1958 the FIA was being 'forced' by the gasolene companies to use more or less ordinary pump fuel as they felt that its use in racing would be a sales boost for their products. It was, therefore, decided that 130 octane 'Avgas' aviation fuel would be used from 1958. This was no problem for Ferrari as his formula 2 cars had run on normal fuel so development of the basic unit would be easy while other contenders for the formula 1 crown would have to convert their engines from alcohol-based fuels.

In September 1957 at the Modena Grand Prix Collins and Musso had two formula 2 cars but engines bored out from 1500 to 1860cc. Both cars performed well even if neither won. The next stage was at the Moroccan Grand Prix when two new units were tried out. Hawthorn's had a capacity of 2195cc while Collins had the full-blown engine for 1958 with a displacement of 2417cc. After 10 laps Hawthorn retired with engine trouble and Collins spun twice, on the second occasion damaging the nose too badly to continue.

The front-engined Dino 246 formula 1 had a full season of racing in 1958 starting with the South American events, the Argentine and Buenos Aires Grand Prix, when three cars were available for the first race and a fourth car, which was late in arriving, was available for the second race. Luigi Musso posted two seconds while Hawthorn had a third in the Argentine Grand Prix.

Except in the Dutch and German Grand Prix the 246 F1 had a reasonable, if not good season, winning five races and finishing either second or second and third in the others. For the two last grands prix of the season the 256 F1 made its appearance – von Trips driving one in the Italian Grand Prix at Monza and Mike Hawthorn in the Moroccan race on 19 October using the same car.

A number of modifications were carried out on the formula 1 cars for 1959. Coil spring rear suspension with Koni telescopic dampers was now standard on all cars and by this time Ferrari had been convinced that disk brakes were superior to the drum so Dunlops were fitted. Dunlop tires also replaced the

Engleberts. The body received attention from Fantuzzi who gave it a slimmer line with high cockpit sides and a longer tail.

The annual South American races had been cancelled so the season started in Europe with two races in England. The Aintree '200' for formula 1 cars attracted two Ferraris, the revised Dino 246 F1 for Tony Brooks, and the 256 F1 (which now developed 300bhp) for Jean Behra. Due to various retirements Behra came out the winner at 88.76mph followed home by Tony Brooks. At Silverstone, for the Daily Express Trophy, Tony Brooks and Phil Hill drove the 246 F1s but only Hill finished and he was fourth. Brooks had a reasonable season winning the European Grand Prix, held at Reims on 5 July and also the German Grand Prix.

Places were obtained in the remaining championship races for 1959 so the season was not quite fruitless although the Dinos could be said to be in decline. It also seemed strange that more use was not made of the 256 F1 which had won at Aintree and was not fielded again during the season.

1960 was the final season for the front-engined formula 1 cars run by the works and their decline was more noticeable, Ferrari gaining a few places but too many retirements due mainly to drive-shaft and other transmission failures.

The day of the rear-engined Ferrari was about to begin, and to start with,

in 1961, they did it in style. The first Ferrari formula 1 rear-engined car had made its debut in the Monaco Grand Prix, around the houses, as early as 29 May 1960. The prototype incorporated many features of the existing cars including chassis, suspension etc. but the 246 F1 unit was behind the driver. There was a new 5-speed transmission and final drive unit with the disk brakes mounted inboard. The clutch was located in the air-stream at the rear of the car. The car had been put together somewhat hurriedly and its handling was not all that could be desired indicating that the factory had a great deal to learn about suspension when the engine was rear-mounted. However, even on such a twisting road circuit as Monte Carlo, Richie Ginter who had the drive did bring the car home in 6th place.

The Tipo 156 F1

While the front-engined Dino 246 was in its last throes in opposition to the British rear-engined cars during 1960 work had been in progress at Maranello in preparation for the 1.5-liter formula to become effective on 1 January 1961. Carlo Chiti was, in the main, responsible for the design of the 156 F1 and it became an immediate success.

It was often the case that Ferrari refused to be rushed into new innovations – such as disk brakes, rear-mounted engines etc. – until he had convinced himself that they were workable. But he was always ready for any new regulations set out by the FIA. For 1961 he would be prepared while the British constructors, who were arguing with the authorities over the new formula, would be left behind as they had convinced themselves that they had a good case for its postponement.

The new Ferrari had a 65 degree V6 unit with four overhead camshafts and had similarities to the Jano V6 formula 2 engine of 1957. A 5-speed transmission was in unit with the final drive with the clutch assembly at the very rear and the disk brakes inboard. With minor alterations the first car used the chassis of the rear-engined Monaco car (1960) with particular attention being paid to the suspension as the early chassis had shown poor handling qualities. After satisfactory tests at Modena von Trips was sent with the 156 F1 for the 142-mile Solitude Grand Prix on 24 July 1960, which he won from Lotus and Porsche at 102.22mph.

Some minor detailed changes were carried out over the winter and the works had every hope of a good 1961 season with a great line-up of drivers – Phil Hill, Wolfgang von Trips, and Richie Ginther with Willy Mairesse and Ricardo Rodriguez as reserves. The most striking feature of the cars was the shark-like twin-nostril nose which was to be noted also on the sports prototype cars of the time.

The first appearance of the 156 F1 was at Siracuse when a car loaned to the Italian Federation of Scuderias Automobile (a mixture of various Italian racing teams) and driven by Giancarlo Baghetti won the 56 lap race to everyone's surprise. He performed the same feat at Posillipo (Naples Grand Prix) on 14 May!

While changes had been made to the 156 F1 during the winter, work was also proceeding on a new lighter version V6 engine. The V had been widened to 120 degrees which improved the overall balance of the engine and at the same time gave a lower center of gravity resulting in a lower body-line. Weber had produced a new twin-choke carburetor for the wide-angled engine, the 40 IF3C, giving a power output of 190bhp at 9500rpm.

The works entered 65 degree cars for Phil Hill and von Trips and a 120 degree car for Richie Ginther at Monaco on 14 May. While Ginther was pushing Moss (Lotus) very hard over the last part of the race he just failed to beat him to the finish line, being 3 seconds behind with Hill third and von Trips fourth; not a bad beginning. The season progressed with four championship victories for the 120 degree engine and one (the French Grand Prix at Rheims) for the 65 degree unit. The Dutch event was a one-two placing while at Spa Francorchamps (Belgian Grand Prix) a clean sweep for all four Ferraris (three 120 degree followed by a 65 degree car). It was fortunate that Hill won the 'home ground' event at Monza as three of the marque cars retired and von Trips was fatally injured on lap 2 when he and Jim Clark collided.

The winter of 1961 was one of dissent and discontent. Chief engineer Carlo Chiti and team manager Tavoni together with other senior staff walked out. No light has ever been thrown on the row which culminated in this unprecedented happening but it did mean that vital work came to a standstill.

1962 proved a difficult year for the factory as most of the cars were updated 1961 models and the only important development was a 6-speed transmission and an experimental 65 degree engine with a displacement of 1480cc used by Willy Mairesse for the Brussels Grand Prix. Mairesse was not exactly an exemplary driver, being more of a 'harum scarum' type and lived up to his reputation in the race, spinning off and not being averse to 'knocking off' his rivals. He won!

Due to industrial troubles in Italy Ferrari missed the French Grand Prix and also a formula 1 race at Reims but was back for the German Grand Prix at the Nurburgring where one car was new with a multi-tubular chassis built from lighter and smaller diameter tubing. The engine and 6-speed transmission

with the outboard clutch were retained. The frontal area had been greatly reduced by the use of a reclined driving position which meant moving forward the steering box and track rods to give the drivers' feet and pedals more room. Following Lotus practise the chassis members carried water to and from the rear-mounted radiator. The body had been redesigned with slim fuel tanks on either side of the cockpit. The former twin-nostril nose had been abandoned and it was now an oval opening and much shorter. Phil Hill was supposed to have the car but found he slid down too far each time he tried it! So Bandini had the drive, Phil Hill and Baghetti 120 degree cars and Rodriguez a 65 degree model. The new Ferrari did not do well with the older car taking 6th place with Baghetti 10th. Bandini crashed and Hill retired with handling problems.

Generally the Scuderia had a very moderate season including a poor Monza where Ferrari always hopes to do well. Phil Hill had become disenchanted with the cars and Maranello generally. Never an easy man to deal with he never did understand the Italians nor could he grasp the fact that Ferrari put his cars first and drivers a poor second. After all he must have known the score for he had been driving the sports racing cars before he was promoted to the formula cars. On the other hand the 156 F1 was now passé and very little had been done in the way of any real revision. Anyway he left the Scuderia but Ferrari had his new number one driver already lined up in the person of John Surtees, and one of the very few motorcyclists to succeed on four wheels.

1963 saw a further revision of the 156 F1 with a rear suspension which followed that of the Lotus but this had to be modified after testing. During the winter further development was undertaken and the car for 1963 came out with an even lighter frame and suspension reverting to the 1962 model.

Rumor had it that Ferrari was not only developing a V8 but also a flat 12 engine and by the spring it had become common knowledge. It would be some time before either was ready so the 156 F1 had to do duty but the Webers were now replaced by Bosch high-pressure fuel injection. The 6-speed transmission was located between the engine and rear axle but was now of a more compact size. The body was redesigned from the one which Bandini had for the German Grand Prix having a longer, tapering nose with a

Left: The 1961 Monaco Grand Prix. Ritchie Ginther got the new 120-degree engined car, while Von Trips (behind) drove a modified 65-degree engine.

Above: John Surtees, ex-world 500cc motorcycle champion, got his first drive for Ferrari in 1963. He took many important wins before moving on to Cooper-Maserati in 1966.

Right: Giancarlo Baghetti in a 156 F1 at Aintree in 1962, one of the worst seasons ever for Ferrari F1 racing.

high sloping tail and the fuel intakes covered by gauze. The roll bar was kept low and it is doubtful whether it would have given the driver much protection if the car had overturned.

The season showed the further decline of the 156 F1 120 degree car. There were too many retirements due to a variety of ailments and apart from Surtees winning the German Grand Prix, the Mediterranean event at Pergusa, and the Rand Grand Prix at Kyalami, there wasn't much to shout about. Surtees did post a second and a third and Bandini a second at Kyalami.

The 158 F1

The V6 unit had been well worked over during the winter and improvements made to the monocoque chassis. At the same time work had been progressing on the new V8 which had undergone tests at Monza in the fall. Despite this the new car was hastily buttoned-up a few days before it made its debut at the Sicilian event at Siracusa on 12 April. Even the bodywork was a trifle rough by Ferrari standards!

Bandini in the V6 led until Surtees' V8 passed him and stayed ahead until the finish. While chasing Arundell (Lotus) Bandini set a new lap record, passed him on lap 37 and went on to take second place.

The 90 degree V8 had a displacement of 1487cc with twin overhead camshafts per bank of cylinders, twin plugs per cylinder and Bosch high-pressure fuel injection. The power output was 220bhp at 11,000rpm. Unfortunately the V8 failed to live up to its first success at Siracusa until Surtees won the German Grand Prix at the Nurburgring on 2 August with a further victory in the Italian Grand Prix. He did, however, have second places at Solitude, Watkins Glen, and the Mexican event at Magdalena Mixhuca, and these placings brought him the Drivers' World Championship. With the exception of the Italian Grand Prix, when Scarfiotti drove a 156 F1 into 10th place and Pedro Rodriguez drove a similar car in the Mexican race, the Scuderia ran a two-car team of Surtees and Bandini throughout 1964.

The long-awaited flat 12 car, the 1512 F1, was on hand at Monza for the Italian Grand Prix, but Ferrari decided that insufficient testing had been done so withdrew the car from the race.

After the Italian event the row which had been brewing between Ferrari and the Italian Automobile Club reached a point of no-return – well at least as long as Ferrari wanted it to continue! The furore was over the non-homologation of the 250 LM as a gran turismo car. 100 had to be built before homologation would be granted for it to compete in the GT category otherwise it had to run as a prototype. The row had, of course, started with the FIA. The result was that Ferrari handed in his competition licence and vowed his cars would never race in Italy again!

In view of all this Ferrari asked Luigi Chinetti of NART to enter and run his 158 F1 and 1512 F1 in the United States and Mexican Grand Prix and they

were to run in the American racing colors of blue and white. Bandini had the flat 12 for both races, retiring with engine trouble at Watkins Glen and finishing third in the Mexican event.

The 1512 F1

The flat 12 had only two outings in 1964 but ran a full season in 1965 driven mainly by Bandini. The South African Grand Prix was now transferred to early January and two cars (the V8 for Surtees and flat 12 for Bandini) were shipped out to East London. Team manager Eugenio Dragoni was nominated as entrant since Ferrari had not, at that time, re-applied for his entrants' competition licence.

Surtees took the V8 to second place but finished a long way behind winner Jim Clark's Lotus. Bandini retired on lap 67.

The 1512 F1 (or 512 F1 as it is also called) had a 180 degree flat 12 engine with a cubic capacity of 1489.6cc. There were two camshafts per bank of cylinders, Lucas fuel injection replaced the Bosch high-pressure unit and ignition was by four coils and distributors. In 1964 there was one plug per cylinder but for 1965 two plugs per cylinder. Compression ratio was 9.8:1 with a power output of 220bhp at 11,500rpm (increased to 225bhp for 1965). Much of the running gear was similar to that of the 158 F1 with the chassis of monocoque structure forming the cockpit and stressed skin compartments for fuel tanks made from riveted sheet steel.

Neither the 158 F1 nor the flat 12 scored a single victory in 1965 although both had reasonable placings in a number of races. After the Italian Grand Prix Surtees took his Lola T70 to the CanAm Canadian Grand Prix where he received terrible injuries when the hub-carrier collapsed during practice. It was thought at the time that he would never race again but he was back again in a racing car by May 1966.

The 312 F1

For 1966 the FIA changed the regulations for formula 1 racing, limiting engine capacities to 3-liters unsupercharged or 1500cc supercharged. It was not unexpected when Ferrari declared that his contender would be a V12 unit – after all he had all the experience in the world to produce a reliable and fast engine with this configuration even if the last 'pure' racing engine had been in 1953. Ing. Rocchi was given the job of designing the engine and he chose to base the design on the 4-liter unit which powered the 330 P3. The 60 degree V12 engine had a displacement of 2989cc and featured twin overhead camshafts per bank of cylinders. Ignition was by two plugs per cylinder with four coils and twin distributors. Lucas fuel injection, similar to the system used by the 1512 F1, fed fuel from a high-pressure pump mounted on top of the engine. With a compression ratio of 11.8:1 the power output was 360bhp at 10,000rpm.

Far left: Lodovico Scarfiotti, who drove for Ferrari in 1963, 1966 and 1967.

Left: Lorenzo Bandini never really got the recognition he deserved, yet drove well for Ferrari for five years from 1962.

Right: Mike Parkes, on his first drive for Ferrari, replacing Surtees for the 1966 French Grand Prix. Ferrari had to build a longer car to accommodate the Englishman's extra height.

Below: Nino Vaccarella at the 1965 Italian Grand Prix. Assigned the V8 car when the new Flat-12 was given to Surtees, he did well until a broken valve ended his race.

Only one of the new models was ready for the season's first race at Siracusa on 1 May with Surtees at the wheel, who duly won. As make-weight Ferrari sent along a Dino V6 which had been prepared for Surtees to use in the Tasman races during the European winter months but Surtees' severe injuries precluded his participation. This car had a 1965 formula 1 V8 chassis with a 2417cc engine and, driven by Bandini, it took second place.

1966 was not all that satisfactory with only two more victories in championship races. John Surtees won at Spa Francorchamps and Scarfiotti won at Monza followed home by Mike Parkes. After the Spa race Surtees was part of the team for the annual Le Mans race but Dragoni, team manager, considered he might not be sufficiently fit for all his stints during the endurance race and brought in Scarfiotti as spare driver. Upset, Surtees walked out and took off for Maranello to see Enzo Ferrari but got no change from him and Surtees left the Scuderia for good. Dragoni never was blessed with tact!

The young New Zealander, Chris Amon, was signed up for 1967 but was unable to take his seat for the Race of Champions at Brands Hatch on 12 March being injured in an accident on the way to the circuit. Bandini took his place in the latest car which now had the exhausts, in an asbestos trough, inside the engine V. Scarfiotti had a normal 1966 model and finished 5th while Bandini made second place.

The Daily Express Trophy at Silverstone was won by Mike Parkes and the only other victory during the season was at Siracusa when Parkes and Scarfiotti with little in the way of opposition toured the circuit and crossed the finish line together to score a dead-heat and a rather hollow victory.

Bandini and Amon were sent to Monaco for the Monte Carlo Grand Prix. On lap 71 the two Ferraris were running second and third but on lap 82 Bandini misjudged a chicane, struck a barrier and the car, out of control, hit the outside straw bales and losing a wheel overturned in the road. The car was righted but suddenly the fuel tank exploded trapping the strapped-in Bandini. He died of severe burns. His death left a great gap in the Ferrari set-up as he was not only a first-rate driver but popular at the works and amongst the Italian enthusiasts.

Three cars were entered for the Belgian Grand Prix for Amon, Parkes and Scarfiotti but they must have felt like many of the other drivers – what chance had they against the sensational new Lotus 49 powered by the V8 Cosworth engine financed by Ford? These cars had made their debut at the Dutch Grand Prix on 4 June. It is interesting to recall that it was at Spa Francorchamps (Belgian GP) that both Brabhams and Ferraris featured the high-mounted rear aerofoils which were to become regular 'wear' on all racing cars for a number of years until they became an integral part of the cars. During the Belgian race Parkes overdid it at the fast left-hander at Blanchimont crashing heavily. This seemed to have unnerved both Amon and

Scarfiotti and the latter, having seen a number of his former team mates killed, decided to quit formula 1 racing. This left Chris Amon to see out the remainder of the season as sole Ferrari representative. A heavy and lonely burden especially as the car was not fully competitive but at least it was pretty reliable. So, for Ferrari there was little to rejoice over during 1967 even though a new V12 engine with four valves per cylinder was produced for the Italian Grand Prix at Monza. Amon could only manage 7th place. Ironically the man who had been discarded by Dragoni a year earlier won the race for Honda – none other than John Surtees!

Jacky Ickx joined Amon for the 1968 season with a little help at the season's end from Englishman Derek Bell and, in the first race at Kyalami, from de Adamich. Once again reliability was the keynote but it doesn't necessarily win races. Ickx did win the French Grand Prix over the Rouen-les-Essarts circuit on 7 July but otherwise he and Chris Amon had to be content with minor placings.

Late in the season the cylinder heads and camshafts were modified and the cars were now pushing 412bhp at 10,500rpm but for all this Amon retired at the Canadian event on 22 September. The United States Grand Prix saw Bell and Amon retiring while a similar situation prevailed at the Mexican Grand Prix – Amon had transmission failure and Ickx engine failure.

Jacky Ickx couldn't see any furtherance in his career by remaining with Ferrari for 1969 so he left to drive for Brabham but he would be back the following year when an entirely new car would be available. So, once more Amon had to play a solo part driving his last race for Ferrari in the British Grand Prix when he retired with transmission problems. For the remainder of the season Pedro Rodriguez drove the 312 F1 V12 but without any luck.

Before the 1969 Italian Grand Prix (Monza) on 7 September it became known that a new Ferrari flat 12 grand prix contender was being tested. It was hoped that it would make its debut in the race but in testing at Modena the engine broke. While there were still three more championship events to be run all were overseas and Ferrari was hardly likely to send a brand new car too far from home in the initial stages so its first race appearance was left until 1970.

The 312 B F1

The power unit of the new 312 B owed its origin to the 1965 1512 F1 (which was never fully developed) and the 2-liter flat 12 of the 212 E 'Montagna' sportscar with which Peter Schetty won the 1969 European Hill Climb Championship. The flat 12 unit was mounted ahead of and drove the rear wheels. Displacement was 2991cc. The crankcase and cylinder blocks were aluminum alloy and the twin overhead camshafts per bank of cylinders were gear driven, operating two exhaust and two inlet valves. A single plug was ignited

Left: Monza in 1966. Scarfiotti became the first Italian to win since Ascari's victory in 1952. He also recorded the fastest lap.

Right: Chris Amon at the French Grand Prix in 1967, where he managed third place until the 48th lap when his throttle pedal came adrift.

Below: The impressive flat-12 312 B formula 1 car. New for the 1970 season, the engine was extremely over-square and ran only four main bearings on a solid billet crankshaft.

by a Marelli transistor and fuel fed by Lucas injection. Compression ratio at 11.8:1 gave a power output of 455bhp at 11,500rpm. Transmission was via a dry multi-plate clutch between the engine and 5-speed transmission which was in unit with the final drive.

Ickx now back with Ferrari found he was the only driver for the South African Grand Prix where he retired with a loss of oil. He was also on his own at Jarama for the Spanish event where he crashed and also at Monte Carlo (Monaco GP) where he had drive-shaft failure. Not a good beginning! Things were to improve.

At Spa Francorchamps (Belgian GP) Giunti joined Ickx but the breakthrough did not happen until the Austrian Grand Prix at Osterreichring on 16 August which Ickx won at 129.27mph, followed home by Clay Regazzoni (now a regular team member) with Giunti 7th. This was followed by Regazzoni's win in the Italian Grand Prix at 147.07mph although Ickx and Giunti retired with engine and transmission troubles respectively. Finally, in the Mexican Grand Prix, Ferrari scored a one-two for the second time in the season. So a poor start finished in a total vindication of the new model.

After the euphoria of the 1970 end-of-season races it was not surprising that 1971 also started on a high note with victories in the first three races entered and a 2nd in the Spanish Grand Prix. This was followed by Ickx winning the Jochen Rindt Gedachtnis-Rennen at Hockenheim on 13 June. By the time of the Dutch event Ickx and Regazzoni had the revised semi-monocoque cars with new bodywork – the 312 B2. Ickx won with Regazzoni 3rd. The rest of the season would best be forgotten for the 312 B2 suffered mainly from engine failure but reliability was again found for the Canadian Grand Prix, even if two cars finished down the line while Regazzoni crashed.

For 1972 the 312 B2 power output was boosted to 480bhp at 12,500rpm. Unfortunately all the work carried out was fruitless with only a single victory at the Nurburgring on 30 July with Ickx leading Regazzoni home and Merzario in 12th place.

Early in 1973 the 312 B3 was ready with a full monocoque chassis and side-mounted radiators ahead of the rear wheels which was later changed to a single front-mounted radiator in the nose. Then later in the season the monocoque was revised with the radiators located behind the front wheels. A high air scoop was added behind the driver.

It seemed that after the initial appearance of the 3-liter 312 B3, nothing would go right and 1973 was no better than the previous season. Generally speaking there was reliability but speed and handling were lacking.

1974 saw the return of Regazzoni to the team and the signing of Niki Lauda, an Austrian. It was a reasonably fruitful time and the partnership lasted four years. A new team manager was appointed, Luca Montezemolo, a law student aged 25 who had had some experience with the Lancia Rally Team. It was his job – and he did it well – to combine all the elements of the racing team into a coherent unit and he alone would be responsible for reporting back to Enzo Ferrari. During the winter of 1973 some intensive work was carried out on the 312 B3. The driving seat was moved forward and an additional fuel tank placed between the seat and engine which put more weight on the front. Alterations were made to the front airfoil and a variety of rear airfoils were available for the season, as different types were required depending on the race circuit. In fact a real touch of professionalism had now crept into the organization, something which had been lacking for many years.

Left: Ferrari had three 312 Bs at Barcelona for the 1971 Spanish Grand Prix. Ickx, Regazzoni and Andretti drove.

Above: Lauda at Monaco in 1974. Number 12 was trucked in from Maranello overnight after he'd wrecked the first one in practice. Sadly he coasted to a halt on lap 33 with suspected ignition trouble, though the fault was never found.

Right: The 1973 version of the 312 BB formula 1 car with totally new chassis, which caused the car to become known as 'The Snowplow.' The wheelbase was only 93 inches (236cm).

The first championship race of the season was the Buenos Aires City Grand Prix and while not in the winner's enclosure, Lauda, in his first Ferrari race, posted a second with Regazzoni third. Two weeks later at Interlagos Regazzoni went one better and came second. Lauda retired on lap 2 with a broken fender. The most promising race during the first half of the season was at Jarama for the Spanish event which was a one-two result with Lauda winning, followed home by Regazzoni. Another one-two was posted at Zandvoort. Lauda taking the chequered flag. Lauda also took a 2nd at Dijon for the French Grand Prix with Regazzoni in attendance third.

Regazzoni won at the Nurburgring, Lauda having an accident before completing a lap. The rest of the season was not so successful but on the whole Ferrari must have been quite pleased.

The 312 B3 was still used early in the 1975 season for the South American races; both drivers scored championship points but their placings were low.

The 312 T F1

By the time the South African Grand Prix came round on 1 March 1975 both drivers had the new 312 T although a 312 B3 was also shipped out. Its debut was not spectacular with Lauda doing no better than 5th and Regazzoni having to retire on lap 71 with a broken throttle linkage.

However, before the next championship round, Lauda was at Silverstone for a non-championship race which he won.

After all the traumas during the development of the 312 B3 Ferrari was to strike gold with the 312 T. It had a completely new monocoque chassis but more importantly it had a transverse 5-speed transmission developed for the new car. The letter 'T' after 312 stood for *transversale*. While this new layout gave a better weight distribution it also gave an efficient power flow alleged to be far in excess of the normal type transmission. This was shown by the power output which was 500bhp at 12,000rpm.

The whole concept of the body was concentrated on its aerodynamic shape giving a better airflow both over and beneath the body.

After the South African Grand Prix and the minor Silverstone race the European season started in earnest at Barcelona on 27 April with the Spanish event. A number of drivers had decided to forgo the race protesting that the safety precautions were inadequate. Lauda and Regazzoni started qualifying one-two on the grid. Andretti's Parnelli clouted Regazzoni's car on lap 1 knocking it into Lauda's 312 T. Lauda had to retire and Regazzoni went out on lap 11.

The Monaco, Zolder, and Anderstorp races were next on the calendar and Niki Lauda was first over the finishing line in all three giving him a good lead in the Drivers' Championship which he was not to lose.

At Zandvoort Lauda failed to catch James Hunt (Hesketh) by one second but reversed the placing at the Paul Ricard circuit. A multiple pile-up at Silverstone resulted in half the 26 field being eliminated but although both Ferraris finished no points were scored.

Lauda should have won the German Grand Prix at the Nurburgring. A front tire puncture about half-way round the long circuit meant he had to get back to his pit on the wheel rim for a change of wheel. However, he scored a further four points for coming in third and once again the irrepressible Regazzoni set a lap record before falling oil pressure led to his motor blowing up. A really wet Austrian Grand Prix over the Osterreichring saw Lauda, who had started on pole, leading for 15 laps but his suspension, as set, could not stand up to the almost awash track, allowing other cars to overtake him. The race was stopped around the halfway mark and with a shortened race distance the 'points finishers' only got half their normal marks!

At the non-championship Swiss Grand Prix (held in Dijon as the Swiss do not approve of motor racing), Regazzoni won with ease.

Ferrari always tried to make Monza his set piece and loud and long are the wails of the partisan Italian fans and national press if the performance of his cars do not come up to their expectations. As the season had so far shown, the 312 T was the car to beat and it was an hysterical crowd who came to watch as Lauda and Regazzoni were side-by-side at the front of the grid. Regazzoni led from start to finish with Lauda following him for 45 of the 52 laps when a rear shock absorber let him down and Fittipaldi moved up into second place. Lauda, however, hung on to 3rd place and clinched the Drivers' title. Regazzoni also set the fastest lap of the meeting for Ferrari.

Below left: Lauda's 312 T at Monaco in 1975. He went out with no oil pressure (at one point he was declutching in the turns!) and Regazzoni finally crashed at the chicane.

Right: For the first time, the Americans had a second Grand Prix in 1976. This is the Long Beach 'street' circuit with Regazzoni leading from the start for a fine win.

Below: Regazzoni again, this time at Monaco in 1976. Driving the long-awaited 312 T2, he finally hit the rails after a tussle with Scheckter.

To end an excellent season Lauda won the USA Grand Prix at Watkins Glen, so the factory won the Manufacturers' championship as well, having scored six victories in 14 championship races, added to which were two non-championship wins.

Ferrari unveiled the 312 T2 in October 1975 but it showed few changes from the original 312 T apart from a slightly shorter wheelbase. The revised car also had to conform with two new regulations. Fender dimensions were limited and the tall, ungainly looking airboxes were taboo. These edicts had to be complied with as from the Spanish GP.

For 1976 the 312 T did good service until the newer car made its debut at Jarama on 2 May for the Spanish event. Lauda had won at Interlagos and Kyalami and Regazzoni had led from start to finish at Long Beach!

The 312 T2s looked a much neater job with the removal of the high air-scoops. There were now two NACA-type scoops ahead of and on either side of the windshield which ducted air along the sides of the cockpit to the two boxes of six fuel-injection trumpets.

Lauda could only post a second at Jarama but a dispute over the wing width of James Hunt's winning McLaren promoted Lauda to first (to be re-versed a little later). Everything seemed to be going Ferrari's way again but the winning streak began to falter at Anderstorp (Lauda was 3rd) and although finishing 2nd at Brands Hatch Lauda was promoted to first as James Hunt's McLaren had been worked on during the interval between the stopping of the race (a first lap accident) and its re-start. This, of course, led to the usual protest. In fact disputes on a variety of matters were now creeping into the grand prix scene and over the years have brought motor racing at the top level into disrepute, with 'cheating' being quite common, albeit that the 'cheating' has crept in due to the interpretation constructors have placed on some of the more loosely worded regulations, and if there are loop-holes then those in authority are to be blamed.

All that is as may be after a near-fatality occurred at the Nurburgring on 1 August when Lauda crashed on lap 2. There can be little doubt that the ghastly accident was due to lack of tire adhesion. The circuit was both wet and dry and Lauda was on slicks. The car caught fire and it was only due to the combined efforts of drivers such as Lunger, Edwards, Ertl and Merzario that he was pulled clear of the raging inferno. Given a 50/50 chance of living

Lauda finally survived and it says much for his will power that he was back driving a Ferrari in the Italian Grand Prix some six weeks later!

No doubt shocked by the accident the factory did not prepare a car for Regazzoni for the Austrian event. Since Lauda was recovering the lack of an entry didn't really make much sense. With Lauda out of action and Ferrari no doubt thinking he wouldn't race again during the season, he decided to put Carlos Reutemann (who had left the Brabham outfit) under contract. However, Lauda was ready for the Monza race so three cars were fielded. Lauda took 4th place while Regazzoni was second to Peterson's March.

With Lauda's recovery and the signing of Reutemann, Ferrari made an extremely unpopular move – he discarded Regazzoni for 1977. Regazzoni was always popular not only among his fellow drivers but with the Italian fans and gentlemen of the press.

With the circus moving over to the North American continent, Ferrari had no answer to James Hunt who won both the Mosport (Canadian) and Watkins Glen (USA) events which left Lauda three points ahead of Hunt (68-65) before the final grand prix at Fuji (for the Japanese GP). The race was another fiasco (too many races had turned out to be a travesty of what motor racing should be about during the season). At Fuji visibility was almost nil due to the really appalling weather. It was not really surprising when Lauda decided to call it a day having completed two laps. After all he had had a traumatic season. As Hunt took third place scoring 4 points he pipped Lauda by one point to win the Drivers' championship.

1976 was not a season when anyone could be proud with all the stupid quibbling that had accompanied so many of the events. In fact it was grand prix racing at its worst!

Ferrari, quite naturally, had not been overpleased at Lauda's retirement at Fuji and there can be little doubt that this caused the somewhat brittle and delicate relationship between the two men to break into open conflict before the end of the 1977 season.

All kinds of minor adjustments were made over the winter and during the new season, including moving the driver to a more forward position, revised air intakes and redesigned rear fender mount.

Reutemann and Lauda formed the team up to and including the USA race at Watkins Glen when Lauda decided that he had had enough of going round in circles. His relationship with Ferrari and the factory had reached a new low and it was not until he failed to practice for the Canadian event at Mosport that the motor racing world knew he had quit and agreed to drive for Brabham. Ferrari was, of course, prepared and brought in young Gilles Villeneuve to partner Carlos Reutemann at Mosport where he was awarded 12th place although not running at the finish. At Fuji he had an accident on lap 5 and retired.

Lauda, before leaving the Scuderia, had enjoyed a reasonable season with three championship victories and a number of high placings which enabled him to win back the Drivers' title, so narrowly lost the previous season.

The early 1978 races were, as usual, held in South America and while Villeneuve did put in the fastest lap at Buenos Aires he could only finish 8th to Reutemann's 7th. At Rio Reutemann won and so ended the life of the 312 T2 to be replaced at Kyalami (South African GP) by the 312 T3. Both drivers retired on lap 55.

Although the 312 T3 was very different from its predecessor it had many of the details which had been tested out on the 1977 cars, but visually the difference was apparent.

The wheelbase was adjustable from 2560 to 2700mm by using various sets of front A-arms. Its track dimensions were also the widest of any of the cars yet built – front 1620mm, rear 1585mm.

1978 was a moderate season for the factory although the new car made first place on four occasions – at the West Coast Grand Prix won by Reutemann, the British Grand Prix also won by Reutemann, the USA event (Reutemann again) and on his home ground at Montreal in the Canadian GP Gilles Villeneuve achieved his first championship win.

There can be no doubt that the 312 T3 was a reliable car and its performances during the 1978 season were in the main spoiled by the poor quality of the Michelin tires which just could not stand the pace. In spite of this it is doubtful whether the T3 could have withstood the assault of the Lotus 79 which, when on form, was certainly devastating.

Left: Lauda driving another in the 312 T2 series for the 1977 season.

Above right: The all-new 312 T3 at Monaco in 1978. Gilles Villeneuve drove the Number 12 car before he dumped it on the guardrails at the chicane.

Right: Carlos Reutemann at Brands Hatch for the British Grand Prix in 1978 where he took the checkered flag for Ferrari in front of Lauda.

Reutemann left the Scuderia at the end of 1978 and was replaced by South African Jody Scheckter. Reutemann had served his term well with the team but perhaps he was too much of a loner; caution was a word which would have best described him. He was not a pursuer, especially if he felt any situation was more or less hopeless!

As for several years past Ferrari relied on his previous season's model to set the scene in South America for 1979. The 312 T3 failed to produce at either track although Villeneuve was 5th and Scheckter 6th in Brazil. In its final appearance Villeneuve won a non-championship race at Brands Hatch.

It was no less a person than Enzo Ferrari himself who described the 312 T4 as the ugliest formula 1 car ever produced by the factory. It was the first Ferrari designed as a fender car and like its contemporaries was slab-sided with a skirted mid-section. Somehow the front fender seemed out on a limb having nothing to do with the rest of the bodywork.

Ugly or handsome the T4 showed its paces to good effect at both Kyalami on 3 March and Long Beach (USA) on 8 April when Villeneuve and Scheckter posted a one-two in each race and in that order.

Scheckter then showed his form by winning at Zolder and Monaco and with a reliable car managed to take the Drivers' Championship by winning at Monza on 9 September with team mate Villeneuve following him home.

The 312 T4 rounded off its career at Watkins Glen when Gilles Villeneuve won the USA Grand Prix after finishing in second place on his home ground at Montreal.

The V6 Turbocharged 126 C

Often at Maranello an entirely new concept got 99 per cent attention and the current model given scant attention. By 1980 Ferrari was finished with the boxer configuration for racing and his weight was behind the V6 turbocharged 126 C which would be the 1981 contender from the factory.

The turbo-supercharger has been in evidence for a greater part of the twentieth century and it became generally known as the shortened 'turbocharger'. Its popularity, if it may be so called, has latterly been pioneered by Porsche who used such cars in the CanAm series to great effect.

Ferrari had obviously been keeping a wary eye on the performances of the Renault turbocharged formula 1 cars, noting their strengths and weaknesses and as in earlier years played a wait and see game before his engineering team had mastered the technique so that his cars would be an improvement on the Renaults.

It was in 1978 that the factory looked at the possibility of producing a 1.5-liter turbocharged engine and by 1979 a detailed design for a 120 degree V6 unit had been decided upon. In June 1980 the new car, designated 126 C, was shown to the press. The twin overhead camshafts per bank of cylinders were gear-driven and operated two intake and two exhaust valves per cylinder; with a KKK turbocharger, Lucas fuel injection and the one plug per cylinder was sparked by a Marelli transistor. The power output was 540bhp at 11,000rpm. The aluminum monocoque chassis with fiberglass body panels had side fairings which gave aerodynamic downforce, with sliding skirts.

The front suspension had upper rocker arms with inboard shock absorber units and coil springs. There were wide-based lower A-arms and an anti-roll bar. At the rear the half-shafts had constant velocity joints, upper rocker arms and inboard shock absorber units with coil springs, lower links and anti-roll bar.

Apart from the KKK turbocharger, the Comprex (pressure-exchange system) was also tried out as it gave as much power as the KKK but importantly gave reduced throttle-lag, always a problem in the early days.

At the end of 1980 the future of formula 1 racing was in a state of flux. Goodyear had pulled out, leaving a number of teams looking for new tires and the FISA/FOCA conflict was still unresolved and at one time it seemed that each side would try to organize its own series of races. FOCA reached an agreement at the Ferrari works on 19 January (the Maranello Agreement) which then had to be approved by the sporting authorities at FISA. The so-called Concorde Agreement was signed by both parties in Paris on 4 March. A somewhat uneasy settlement had been reached.

Due to all this nonsense the South African Grand Prix (which couldn't be postponed from its original date – 7 February) took place without the FISA-faithful teams such as Ferrari and the result was not recognized as a qualifying event by the FISA.

The San Marino race at Imola was elevated to championship status for 1981 and Villeneuve had a new car with an extended wheelbase lengthened by the insertion of a 5-inch spacer in the shape of an aluminum casting between the engine and transmission – the bodywork being suitably lengthened. The scrutineers had a field day sticking rigidly to the rule book. Out went hydro-pneumatic suspensions, flexible skirts, and flexible strips used to bridge the gap between sidepods and rear wheels! Just about every car, including the Ferraris, was illegal in one way or another. The usual pit lane politicians had a wonderful time. However, a compromise was reached – hydro-pneumatic systems could stay but skirts had to be made of rigid material!

Both cars proved their reliability but that was all.

Two weeks later at Zolder for the Belgian Grand Prix the cheating on skirts was carried to further lengths. Most teams had by now equipped their cars with adjustable ride height systems and FISA had clarified the 6 centimeter rule which was naturally ignored by all. The cheat was to have cockpit control of the ride height – so on entering the pit area the ride height was in the 'up' legal position but once on the circuit in the 'down' position. During the race the Ferraris still showed their reliability but handling was the main problem – in fact the cars required a chassis man but attention to handling and the proper setting up of the cars was still some way off. It was during the 1980 season that the Ferraris acquired the somewhat insulting but nevertheless warranted name of 'moving chicanes'!

After the Monaco race the factory announced that Dr Harvey Postlethwaite would be joining the design team which must, at least, have put some heart into Ferrari supporters who were seeing an excellent design being wasted through atrocious handling. What point in a fast, reliable engine if it won't go where it's directed?

The 126 C2

In November Ferrari announced that, for 1982, his cars would run on Goodyear tires. It had seemed to him that the Michelin company had been favoring the Renault team at his expense. Work had also been progressing on the revised car which had a new suspension, new bodywork, and a narrower transmission. The chassis was a slim monocoque constructed in an aluminum-skinned honeycomb material with carbon fiber used for the front and rear bulkheads, the main structure being bonded together with a complete absence of rivets. It was hard to believe that the under-the-skin structure was indeed Ferrari! The engine and twin KKK turbo installation had been tidied up and with further development of the V6 unit the power claimed was 580bhp. The wheelbase had been shortened, the track widened and with a paring in weight it neared the legal minimum of 580kg.

Pironi was sent out to Kyalami with the much modified 126 C which was, in fact, the prototype for the 126 C2. For the last two days of testing two of the new 126 C2s arrived. The first day of testing did not materialize as the drivers took 'industrial action' objecting to the small print on their licences. The trouble was resolved temporarily but serious practice was left to one day. Various problems arose with the new cars and during the race Villeneuve suffered a broken turbo and Pironi struggled through to 18th place completing only 71 of the 77 laps.

After the South African event all appeared sweetness as it seemed that

Left: The 126 C at Monaco in 1981. Ferrari claimed that the C stood for 'Corsa.' The new turbo cars scored a first with Villeneuve at the wheel though he complained that the cars were very hard work to drive.

Right: The 1982 Turbo engine. Around 600bhp at 11,000rpm from 1500cc!

FOCA supremo Bernie Ecclestone and FISA boss Balestre were now the best of chums, but Ecclestone and Enzo Ferrari were at war, with acrimonious letters flying around. The Argentine Grand Prix scheduled for 7 March was cancelled. For the Brazilian event Villeneuve had a new car with modified bodywork as the front fairings were now blended into the sidepods. Villeneuve left the field standing at the start but an error on lap 30 put him out of contention. Pironi was 8th. A new cheating device was thought up for the race by the Brabham and Williams teams. This consisted of a large plastic water bottle filled before scrutineering so as to ensure the car was the legal minimum weight of 580kg before the race but jettisoned during the early laps so as to reduce this weight. The 'war' was still on! Both Ferrari and Renault lodged protests.

The circus next moved to Long Beach where further protests were in evidence. Pironi's Ferrari appeared on the second day of practice with a peculiar looking rear fender consisting of two staggered narrow chord fenders with a central mounting. The whole fender was as wide as the car and was meant to be Ferrari's challenge to the so-called 'water-cooled' brakes. Both cars were fitted with the new fenders and also had nose fenders for the first time. Villeneuve came in 3rd but Ken Tyrrell protested against the new rear wings and was upheld by the same stewards who had passed the new device

in pre-race scrutineering. So the farce of protest and counter-protest proceeded.

The San Marino Grand Prix (at Imola) on 25 April was the first European event and to everyone's surprise Enzo Ferrari turned up for pre-race testing. A week previously the FIA Court of Appeal decreed that the 'water-bottle' ploy was illegal and all cars finishing a race had to comply with the minimum legal weight of 580kg. They also disqualified Piquet and Rosberg from their Brazilian places over the 'water-cooled' brakes protest. Predictably the FOCA reacted in a childish manner and boycotted the race with the exception of Mr Tyrrell and his equipe (he ran his cars under his Italian sponsors' banner) and also the ATS team. The FISA boys (Ferrari, Renault, and Alfa) contested the race and the organizers managed to get a grid of 14 cars. At least it would be a straight fight between Renault and Ferrari which the latter won with a one-two placing.

Zolder for the Belgian Grand Prix was next but when Villeneuve went out to improve his grid position on the last practice session he was killed in a horrifying accident. A lonely Didier Pironi went to Monaco and with a number of the early leaders falling by the wayside found himself in the lead. However, on the final lap he ceased to drive and was awarded second place. After Monaco it was announced that Patrick Tambay would join Ferrari.

Below left: Long Beach in 1981. Pironi's debut was marred only when his new 126 C's engine quit on lap 67.

Right: Pironi was the only Ferrari entrant for Monaco in 1982 and with one lap to go, he found himself in the lead after Patrese spun at the Station Hairpin. But electrical problems brought the car to a halt in the tunnel with the flag almost in sight.

Below: Gilles Villeneuve at Long Beach in 1982. His 126 C2 came in third behind Lauda in the McLaren and Rosberg in the Williams.

Left: The 126 C3 in 1983. Another Dr Harvey Postlethwaite design, it featured a new molded carbon/Kevlar monocoque chassis and a flat bottom, after the banning of side-skirts.

Below left: Rene Arnoux joined the Ferrari team for 1983 but managed only a disappointing tenth in his first outing at the Brazilian Grand Prix.

Right: Arnoux was often regarded as the wild man of the Ferrari team, but he took three wins in 1983 to Tambay's one.

All the teams flew the Atlantic again to meet up in Detroit for the latest grand prix circuit laid out on 2.59 miles of public roads surrounding the Renaissance Center where Pironi made it to the finish line in third place. This event was followed by the Canadian Grand Prix where Pironi was still on his own and was unfortunate to stall on the grid. Ricardo Paletti (Osella) came storming up and hit the Ferrari's rear and succumbed to his injuries. The race was held up and restarted somewhat late. Pironi had to use the spare car which had not been set-up and could only finish in 9th place.

Both Pironi and Tambay did well at Brands Hatch finishing 2nd and 3rd respectively with Niki Lauda well ahead of the field and quite uncatchable. The French Grand Prix at Paul Ricard was somewhat boring with the two Renaults well in control followed by Pironi and Tambay. For the second time in the season tragedy hit the Ferrari team. During the last practice session for the German Grand Prix at Hockenheimring Pironi hit Alain Prost's Renault suffering severe injuries; he recovered only to die in a powerboat accident in 1987. In the race Tambay was driving well and in second place by quarter-distance. By lap 19 he inherited first place when the leader, Piquet (Brabham), made a stupid error. Tambay just drove on to give Ferrari another win.

Ferrari as always wanted to do well before the 'home crowd' at Monza for the Italian Grand Prix on 12 September so it was necessary to field a complete team of two cars. Good drivers not already under contract were not available – at least those who could handle formula 1 cars, so he had to go outside the current circus pilots. Andretti was an obvious choice; he had been under contract to the Scuderia in the past and had recent formula 1 experience. Although under contract to drive in USAC events he was free for the Monza weekend and with Tambay would make a strong team. Although the 126 C2 did not win it made a strong bid for victory and Tambay crossed the finish line second with Andretti third.

The season's final event was at Las Vegas, hardly a grand prix circuit, more like a scalectrix course which should be eliminated from the annual championship. Although Andretti had a USAC event it was possible for him to take in the Las Vegas event but he might as well have stayed away. The 126 C2 was not handling too well and Andretti got all crossed up at a right-hander and found himself in the sand unable to extract his car.

With all the year's traumas the 126 C2 had acquitted itself well and,

although it is always dangerous to speculate where motor racing is concerned, the thought remains – if either Villeneuve had lived or Pironi had not been sidelined would one or the other have emerged as world drivers' champion?

In 1983 the 126 reached its third evolution. Externally it was sleeker, with radiators and heat exchangers shifted rearward, but under the skin was the new composite chassis of Kevlar and carbon fiber. This year the flat bottom rule, which excluded even side skirts, never mind the true ground-effect venturi of earlier years, forced Ferrari to develop the small fins on the rear of the main profile, and the idea was soon to be seen on every other contender in the pits.

On the track, the new car was successful. Patrick Tambay stayed in the team and was joined by René Arnoux. Tambay's early win at San Marino (Arnoux was third) was in a C2, but the C3 took the flag on its second outing, at the German Grand Prix, with Arnoux at the wheel. Tambay retired during that race, but he was close behind Arnoux at the Dutch Grand Prix in a classic Ferrari 1-2. After that, the season went gradually downhill and both drivers retired in the final event of the year in South Africa.

For 1984 there was the final development of this car, the C4. Cooling was moved even further back, accentuating the shape still more strongly. Later in the year, with a longer wheelbase and the radiators moved forward came the final evolution, the C4M2. This car really marked the end of Forghieri's reign as Technical Director, although its style was echoed on later designs.

For 1984, Scuderia Ferrari fielded an Italian driver, the likeable Michele Alboreto. Both he and his team-mate Arnoux were let down by their cars in a season of 12 retirements, and just one victory, Alboreto at Zolder in the Belgian Grand Prix.

Things looked much better at the start of the 1985 season. The new 156/85 saw the turbo V6 engine moving into the 800hp zone, the new computer-designed body was given extra stability by new pull-rod suspension, and the carbon brake disks became the definitive formula 1 equipment for everyone in short order. Aboreto was joined by the swift Stefan Johansson, and the team ran very well. Victories off the pole at Montreal and the Nurburgring for Alboreto helped him lead the points table until just after midseason, and he was toppled at the Austrian Grand Prix. Things went from bad

Above: The British Grand Prix in 1984. The Ferrari 126 C4 pushed out 800bhp thanks to its twin KKK turbos set at 3.2 bar. The drivers managed fifth (Alboreto) and sixth (Arnoux).

Left: Mechanical and development work isn't all spanners and screwdrivers.

Above right: Michele Alboreto winning the 1984 Belgian Grand Prix at Zolder. 1984 was a terrible season for Ferrari, as the new Italian driver, their first for many years, clocked up just this one victory in 16 races.

Right: Gerhard Berger in 1988. Neither Berger nor Alboreto did much in 1988 since the Ferrari could not match the Prost and Senna in their Honda-powered McLarens.

Far right: Michele Alboreto in 1988 before he moved to Tyrell to make way for Nigel Mansell in the Ferrari team.

to worse thereafter, and the team was dogged by a series of retirements due to mechanical failure – seven retirements in twelve starts at six races.

That was the beginning of a truly awful period in formula 1 for the Maranello team. Alboreto's win at the Nurburgring in 1985 was the last Ferrari victory for two seasons and 37 races. The red cars suffered a series of mechanical failures which were inexcusable in Italian eyes; incredibly the time came when a Ferrari retirement was expected in every race. The 1986 car, the F1 86, suffered badly in terms of aerodynamics and handling, and had difficulty meeting the new reduced fuel consumption allowance, even with the KKK turbos replaced by Garretts. Frantic development work throughout the season concentrated on the front suspension and the aerodynamics, but with no noticeable effects. Throughout the season the best the team could achieve was a sprinkling of third places and one second, Alboreto at Osterreichring.

If anything could be worse, 1987 was it. Alboreto, placed eighth in the first event of the year at Rio, finished third at San Marino, retired from the Belgian Grand Prix and took another third at Monaco. But he retired from every event after that until he was placed fourth and then second in the last two events of the year at Fuji and Adelaide. But by then he'd been overshadowed by his new team-mate, the fast and improving Gerhard Berger, who broke the 37-race duck by winning in Japan and Australia. Worse, Berger had finished fourth at Monza, while Alboreto, the team's number one driver, had retired in front of his home crowd.

There is nothing quite as unforgiving as the Italian racing fan, and Alboreto could never be forgiven. His days at Maranello were numbered, although he stayed on for 1988, and he was sharing his drive with Berger rather than leading the team. There was plenty of controversy about the car too; this season saw the arrival of the British engineer John Barnard as the new Technical Director. Under his guidance the longitudinal transaxle, which is aerodynamically better, reappeared, in conjunction with a longer wheelbase. But like everyone else, 1987 was a year spent chasing the Honda-powered Williams team; Mansell and Piquet were the drivers to beat, and no-one could. At least, not until Berger won the last two races, though by then Piquet had taken another world title and Nigel Mansell had caught the eye of Enzo Ferrari.

Rumors that he had actually signed a contract were scotched when he announced he would run again with Williams for 1988. Mansell must have known how hard that would be since the team had lost Honda support when Senna went to McLaren. He spent a year in the wilderness, as did everyone else, while Prost and Senna romped around every race track in the world. With an in-between situation, the last season of turbo racing, Ferrari chose to adapt the 1987 car while developing their new 3.5-liter V12 for 1989. Meanwhile, 1988 was Senna's season, as the McLaren Hondas overpowered all opposition.

That doesn't mean things were all bad for Ferrari, because they weren't. Both Berger and Alboreto consistently qualified well – Ferraris occupied the first two places on the grid at the start of the British Grand Prix. However they couldn't stay there, and race-length reliability was still a major problem. But everything was set to change for 1989, because that year the turbos were out and so was Alboreto. Mansell and Ferrari signed their 1989 contract mid-way through the 1988 season, announcing it in July, and also announcing the new car for 1989. John Barnard's first ground-up design, it was low, sleek, and narrow, featuring a semi-automatic seven-speed transmission, composite body and chassis which was the brainchild of Dr Harvey Postlethwaite, at least in part.

But any pleasure of anticipation for the coming season was severely curtailed by the saddest blow of all, no less shocking for its inevitability. In August of 1988, Il Commendatore finally passed on. Though he had refused to attend a racetrack for the last 30 years of his life, his influence was all-pervading, all powerful, and right up until the last the red cars raced for the man as much as the team, despite his absence.

Above left: Nigel Mansell signed for Ferrari mid-1988 and rewarded them with a victory in his first race of the 1989 season at the Brazilian Grand Prix.

Above: Gerhard Berger at Silverstone in 1988. The six-cylinder, 1496cc engine with its twin lateral Garrett turbochargers and 630bhp at 12,000rpm got them on the first two places on the grid, but just wasn't enough in the race itself.

Right: While Senna won at Silverstone in 1988, Berger managed 9th and Alboreto came in 17th. Hardly what was expected from the cars in red.

The GT Road Cars

The Gran Turismo cars up to 3 liters

There have been few automobile manufacturers who started out by building cars which they raced successfully and from the knowledge gained went on to construct fast and elegant road cars. It is a path not to be recommended unless the constructor has immense faith in both himself and his product.

Ettore Bugatti showed the way, followed by Enzo Ferrari; the other name which comes to mind is Lotus.

Ferrari's beginnings are well chronicled and his early Colombo designed V12 unit was devised with three purposes in mind – an engine for a racing car, a sportscar, and a road car even if in the early days the comforts of the latter for touring were somewhat inadequate in interior design.

The 166 Series

First of the road cars was the 166 Sport but few of these were built and a brochure of the period had a line drawing of a notchback coupe with some provision for back-seat passengers! Touring, it would seem, was the designer and builder of the bodywork.

The V12 engine had a single overhead camshaft per bank of cylinders, a single plug and two distributors. Three Weber 32 DCF carburetors fed the fuel, and transmission was via a 5-speed transmission mated to the engine. Suspension was the usual independent double wishbones with a transverse spring at the front and the rigid axle and semi-elliptic springs at the rear. With a compression ratio of 7.5:1 the power output was 110bhp at 6000rpm.

The 195 Series

Ferrari continued with his usual process when introducing the 195 by enlarging the bore to give a capacity of 2341cc. There were two models – the Sport and the Inter (the road-going car) with a probable production of near 20. While the Sport had three Weber 32 DCF carburetors, the Inter had a single carburetor of the same type and the wheelbase was longer at 2500mm. The power output was 130bhp at 6000rpm.

The 250 Series

It was with this series that Ferrari finally established himself as the manufacturer of high class gran turismo cars. Up to 1953 the works had built a moderate number of cars – about 200 all told. By the time the 250 Series went out of production with the 1964 GTO the figure had risen to between 3000 and 3500. However, the rapid increase was not due solely to the 250s as other models had also been produced in the intervening years.

The 250 Series saw the light of day in March 1952 when a Vignale bodied berlinetta powered by an experimental 3-liter engine was driven out of the factory gates for its first run. As with other models the series was produced in three versions – competition berlinetta, sportscar and gran turismo car.

At the Paris Salon in 1953 Ferrari had two new gran turismo cars on show with differing engine capacities but using a common chassis. The smaller 3-liter tipo 250 Europa was the first of the touring 250 Series and the V12 engine was from the Lampredi long block range. They are, at times, referred to as the 'first series Europa' and their production run was short, some 20 examples being built. Most were coupes bodied by Pinin Farina who also built a spyder body on one chassis. Vignale did the coachwork on two.

The 2963cc engine had a single camshaft per bank of cylinders, a single plug, coil ignition and three Weber 36 DCF carburetors. The 4-speed transmission was in unit with the engine. The power output was 200bhp at 6000rpm.

By late 1954 Ferrari had returned to the Colombo-based V12 unit and with the 250 Europa GT started a long and profitable line of 3-liter 250s. At that time GT racing was about to replace the sportscars so homologation of the series was obtained which led finally to Ferrari's great success in this type of competition.

At the 1956 Geneva show, using the chassis and the engine of the 250 Europa GT, Pinin Farina produced a coupe version and it was intended that the firm would build the coachwork. A few prototypes were produced but in the final analysis some 70 plus of the cars were completed by Carrozzeria Boano. These cars became known as the 'low roof coupes.' By 1957 Carrozzeria Boano had become Carrozzeria Ellena. The new firm produced about 50 bodies on the Ferrari chassis with a higher roof line and called them the 'high roof coupes' to distinguish the styling of the two versions. The body side panels were flat and the bumpers were not for protection but show. Many of the minor components, such as door latches, handles etc. were standard fittings from either the Fiat or Alfa Romeo factories. Up to that time it could be said that these coupes were the most comfortable Ferraris built. Surprisingly neither Boano nor Ellena identified their handiwork on the coachwork.

Pinin Farina had been working during the winter of 1957/58 on a new style coupe for the 250 Series. The first car was shown in June 1958 and production was carried through until 1960 by which time 350 models of the 250 GT Pinin Farina coupes had been built. There had been some changes to the V12 engine during this period. Disk brakes were an optional extra but later became standard when Ferrari was convinced of their superiority over the drum brake.

Previous pages: The unmistakable Testarossa. A massive 78 inches (198cm) wide, it had flip-up headlights and a door mirror that looks like an afterthought.

Left: The 195 S Berlinetta – a 2341cc. The 195 signified the cubic capacity of each cylinder of the V12 engine.

Above: The 250 GT Spyder California was built partly from steel instead of aluminum for extra rigidity. There were many versions with different engines and bodystyles – all among the most collectable of Ferraris.

Right: The later Pininfarina-styled California, debuted at Geneva in 1960, with its shorter wheelbase and wider track.

Going back to the 1956 Geneva show, the Ferrari stand had on display a Boano built cabriolet but at that time the project was dropped and it was left to Pinin Farina to design the finished car. It was not the first 'open' Ferrari as some had been built earlier, but it was the first of a series. Altogether four prototypes were produced before the production model was to be seen at the 1957 Paris Salon. It was a classic of its kind and some 40 were built in the first series.

Besides the cabriolet Pinin Farina designed a second open car, the 250 GT California spyder, bodywork on which was carried out by Scaglietti. Pinin Farina, who was, by now, the main designer for Ferrari, was into the Series II cabriolets by 1959 and by 1962 when they were phased out, a total of around 210 had been built.

All these cars were two-seaters and it seems that Ferrari had awoken to the fact that the family man might appreciate one of his masterpieces.

Two prototypes were started on toward the end of March 1960 and one was used as the course car for the 1960 Le Mans event. Two production models were shown in the fall, one at Paris and the other, a right-hand-drive car, at London. Both showed some new thinking on the styling from the prototypes. The fog lamps had disappeared and so had the louvers in the rear sail panels. The engine and transmission had been moved forward to allow more interior space for the two additional rear seats. The tipo was designated 250 GT 2 + 2. It was a handsome car but unfortunately did not have a wide appeal and it was, of course, overshadowed by the 250 GT short wheelbase berlinetta. Around 900 250 GT 2 + 2s were built before their factory run came to an end in mid-1963.

At the Paris Salon in October 1962 a prototype of what was to become a classic Ferrari was introduced, designated the 250 GT berlinetta. The word Lusso (meaning luxurious or luxury) was added by the motoring press although not accepted by the works. The engine was still the Colombo-based 3-liter V12 set in a 2400mm wheelbase. A second prototype followed with coachwork, as usual, designed by Pinin Farina and built by Scaglietti. The ultimate design was a combination of two very good-looking cars, the front end bearing a similarity to the short wheelbase model and the rear following the lines of the 250 GTO with a slight 'spoiler' effect built into the rear end. The body was steel but the doors, hood and trunk lid, were aluminum. To give an easier ride the telescopic shock absorbers at the rear had concentric 'helper' springs and Watt linkage was employed (as on the GTO) for the rear axle's lateral location. Disk brakes were by now standard wear. The model probably had the best all-round vision up to that time with no quarter lights and the struts for the door, front, and rear windshields gave minimal interference. All told 350 were built until production ceased in 1964.

Perhaps one of the surprising things about the Lusso is the fact that even today excellent used examples do not command a high price.

With the cessation of the Lusso's run so also ended the production of the under 3-liter front-engined V12 Ferraris. They had enjoyed a long innings and without doubt set up Ferrari in a strong financial position. They were fast and reliable cars which could be used either for grand touring or competition.

The V12 front-engined Gran Turismo cars over 3 liters

In the late summer of 1950 Ferrari announced a new model sportscar, the type 340 America. This was the first car, other than the single seaters, to make use of the Lampredi 'long block' V12 engine. With a bore/stroke of 80 x 68mm the displacement was 4101cc.

By the following January, at the Brussels show, the chassis of a gran turismo car was on display and by the Turin show, in the spring, a complete model was available using the 4.1-liter unit of the 340 America. The tipo was known as the 342 America and it used similar equipment to the earlier car. It differed in the fact that the wheelbase was longer and the early models had a 5-speed transmission in unit with the engine. The bodywork was a high-roof Touring coupe but some were similar in appearance to the 250 Europas and 375 Americas. Production was very limited.

Left: The 410 Superamerica chassis sported many bodystyles. Ghia, Pininfarina, Scaglietti and Vignale all built bodies on the 4.9-liter engined chassis. This is one of Pininfarina's.

Above: Lusso for Luxury. The 250 GT Berlinetta Lusso. Plenty of style but plenty of poke too – some 240bhp at 7500rpm.

Right: Very few of these Tipo 500 Superfast models were produced. Maybe three dozen in all of a car that was the top-of-the-range luxury Ferrari in 1965.

By 1953 the 375 America was on view at the Paris Salon and shown at the same time as the 250 Europa, both cars sharing a common chassis. The V12 unit which powered the few cars which were built had a capacity of 4523cc and a power output of 300bhp at 6300rpm. Most of the coupes were designed and built by Pinin Farina.

As a replacement for the 375 America, a chassis/engine of the next 'offering' was introduced at the 1955 Paris Salon to be followed by a complete car at Brussels early in 1956. This was the 410 Superamerica and the last of the line using the Lampredi 'long block' unit. Production was slow with about one car a month and few were built. A variety of bodies was used as Pinin Farina, Boano, Ghia, and Scaglietti all had a hand in their production. The early cars

were on a long wheelbase but by 1957 a shorter wheelbase model was introduced. The engine was all but 5-liters with a 4-speed transmission in unit with the engine.

To replace the 410 Superamerica, Ferrari returned to a bored-out and longer-stroked version of the Colombo-based engine. Displacement was reduced to 3967cc. The new car was designated 400 Superamerica and on display at Brussels in January 1960.

Superfast was on show in Paris in 1956, a coupe design by Pinin Farina on the short wheelbase 410 Superamerica chassis. A wet-sump version of the 410 Sport 4.9-liter engine was used. It was notable for its cantilever-designed roof with no support pillars at the windshield and, following the American trend at that time, had rear end tail fins which did little to enhance its looks. The radiator grille was large and positioned low down.

An 'aerodynamic' coupe was on the stand at the 1960 Turin show. This was Superfast II and once more designed and built by Pinin Farina for his own use. The grille was small and elliptical and the headlights retractable. A second version appeared a year later but with a larger grille and an airscoop on the hood. While the first car had fender skirts, these were not featured on the later car.

Based on the 1960 model and built on a 400 Superamerica chassis Superfast III was on view at Geneva in 1962. The air scoop from Superfast II was retained but a retractable grille cover was added and at the rear slender pillars were used.

Superfast IV also made its appearance in 1962 but changes had been carried out to the coachwork. The retractable headlights were no longer in evidence and the rear wheel-arch covers had been removed.

The 1964 Geneva show saw the introduction of the handsome 500 Superfast, the only model in the series which went into limited production. Between 1964 and 1966 37 were built. The body was a Pinin Farina design showing some resemblance to the earlier Superfast model. The 4963cc engine was based mainly on the Colombo unit and was new but used various components from the 330 GT 2 + 2. The early cars used a 4-speed transmission with overdrive but later this unit was replaced by a 5-speed transmission which was also used by the later 330 GTs.

In 1963 Ferrari had the 330 GT 2 + 2 on the company's stand at the Paris Salon but clothed in a 250 GT 2 + 2 body. At the time it was known as the 330 America, an interim model of which only 50 were built. The 330 GT 2 + 2 Mk 1 with its own coachwork was at the 1964 Brussels show. It had four headlights and its looks departed from the exotic designs the public expected from Ferrari. The V12 engine was Colombo-based with a capacity of 3967cc and a power output of 300bhp at 6600rpm. While it might not have looked like a Ferrari, it certainly behaved like one for it was extremely fast and very reliable and the back-seat passengers had more room than might have been expected in a 2 + 2. The early cars had a 4-speed transmission and overdrive but later ones were equipped with a 5-speed transmission. After an initial production run of 625 the Mk II version was marketed. This model reverted to the normal, for those days, two headlights and retained the 5-speed transmission. The Mk II had a run of 460 when it went out of production in 1967.

While the 330 GT 2 + 2 was still coming from the factory one of the most handsome designs conceived by Pinin Farina was put on show at the Paris Salon in 1964. It was the 275 GTB and would be the last single overhead camshaft berlinetta built. It was also the first road-going Ferrari to have fully independent rear suspension. A spyder version, the 275 GTS, was also available using the same 3.3-liter power plant. Pinin Farina styled both bodies but the GTB was built by Scaglietti while the GTS was built by the designer. Pinin Farina's styling of the GTS was functional without being exotic, taking a leaf from his design of the 330 GT 2 + 2.

The buyer could, for the first time, have optional extras for the GTB – instead of three Weber 40 DCZ/6 or 40 DFI/1 carburetors, six Weber 40 DCF/6s could be fitted. Also for the first time on a gran turismo car Campagnolo alloy wheels were standard but the buyer could elect to have Borrani wires. The GTS had three Webers and Borranis and there were no options.

A second series GTB was shown at Frankfurt in 1965. As a cover for the carburetors there was a bulge on the bonnet, the vent wing on the driver's window was absent and there was more room for luggage. At the Paris Salon, only a month later, the front styling had been lengthened and such models are known as the 'long nosed' 275 GTB. The model seemingly underwent a number of changes during its life, some minor for styling purposes

and some modifications to the engine. In 1966 at Paris a revised 275 GTB was introduced. For the first time each bank of cylinders had two overhead camshafts but in other respects the new dry-sump engine followed the earlier layout with a single plug, coil ignition, and six Weber carburetors. The 5-speed transmission was in unit with the differential. The revised car was designated 275 GTB/4.

The 275 GTBs showed clearly that when Ferrari produced the 250 GT berlinetta Lusso and the 330 GT 2 + 2, he was getting further away from the 'old style' GT models which were, in reality, thinly disguised racing cars with minimum creature comforts. The Lusso, the 330 and 275 GTB were more civilized cars and even the styling was getting away from the more functional (although still exotic) bodywork of the competition cars. Comfort and good rideability would be the norm for the gran turismo cars of the future.

To many Ferrarists the 330 GTC is the most civilized of the range of gran turismo models and the best road car. First shown at Geneva in March 1966 it used the 275 GTB chassis and the 4-liter engine of the 330 GT 2 + 2. As a styling exercise Pinin Farina decided on the front end of the 400 America, combining this with the rear end of the 275 GTS, and the result was an extremely handsome and elegant automobile. Although using the earlier 330's power unit the cylinder blocks had been redesigned as the GTC's 5-speed transmission was mounted in unit with the differential. Suspension was, of course, all independent. As an optional extra, air-conditioning could be installed. Some 600 models had been produced when it was taken out of production in 1968.

While the 330 GTC had been introduced in the spring of 1966 at Geneva a spyder model, the 330 GTS, came later in the year at the Paris fall Salon. It was to be a replacement for the 275 GTS but after 100 or so examples had been built by Pinin Farina (who was also the designer) production ceased.

Right: Cast alloy wheels had become standard for this 1967 version of the 330 GTC. Sold as a 2+2, the GTC was launched at Geneva in 1966 but was replaced a year later by the 365 version.

Below: Another Pininfarina design, the 365 GT 2+2 was the first Ferrari to incorporate power steering and air conditioning as standard for the US market. The Borrani wires were an option, though. Some 800 were produced between 1967 and 1971.

Alongside the 330 GTC at the Geneva show in 1966 Ferrari presented the last of what might be termed his large-engined luxury cars. It was a spyder and designated 365 California. The V12 engine had a single camshaft per bank of cylinders and displaced 4390cc. There doesn't seem to have been any real point in its manufacture and after 14 models had been built the tipo was abandoned. Perhaps it was a preliminary run for the 365 GT 2 + 2 which appeared in 1967 at the Paris Salon. The same engine was used and the power output of 320bhp at 6600rpm was the same. However, the 5-speed transmission was mated with the engine whereas the 365 California's transmission was in unit with the differential. Pinin Farina designed and built the 800 or so models, the last of which came from the factory in early 1971.

Ferrari was certainly keeping his expanding market going, for, apart from the highly popular and saleable Dino 246 GT, the larger models coming from the factory were filling a void which had not really been exploited – the exotic market.

A sensation was caused at the October 1968 Paris Salon when Enzo Ferrari uncovered a model which could rightly be called a legend even during the period of its production. Although it was designated Tipo 365 GTB/4 it was immediately dubbed the Daytona and is so called today. It was not only the most expensive Ferrari to come from the factory but for a number of years was the fastest road car ever built with a genuine 174mph tag! The engine had twin overhead camshafts to each bank of cylinders with a capacity of 4.4-liters, a single plug per cylinder, and coil ignition. Six Weber 40 DCN 20 carburetors fed the fuel and the power output was 320bhp at 7500rpm. There was dry sump lubrication and there was a 5-speed transmission in unit with the differential. Pinin Farina designed and built the prototype but Scaglietti was detailed to build the production models. Early cars had all the front lights placed behind a full width wrap-around plastic cover but in mid-1971 paired retractable headlights became standard. Although the model caused a sensation when it appeared, there were those to whom the styling was not all that appealing with its long front end, a shortish driving

compartment and Kamm-type rear end. However, the styling was functional and aggressive looking and it was somewhat heavy weighing in at an impressive 3600lbs.

A spyder version, the 365 GTS/4 was shown a year later at Frankfurt. A really beautiful design by Pinin Farina, it had been intended to build a very limited edition – only 15. The final figure was around 150. The design was so popular that many owners with the berlinetta have had the top removed, converting them to spyders.

The 365 GTC and GTS models were introduced in 1969 and were similar in many respects to the 330 GTC except that the engine was a 4.4-liter unit. Two years later a twin overhead camshaft model appeared but it had a short run with some 500 cars produced. Both were designed and built by Pinin Farina and from the experience of owners who tried both models most would agree that the single camshaft tipo was the better car. Both models, however, were in the range of the Ferrari luxury class. The cars were followed by another 2 + 2, the first for some time, designated 365 GT4. Using the same 4.4-liter engine with twin overhead camshafts it had the same power output of 320bhp and like its predecessor the rear suspension was equipped with hydropneumatic self-leveling. There were over 470 units built during quite a long lifespan from 1972 to 1976. This model was also undoubtedly in the luxury class.

With a number of elegant luxury models coming from the factory in quick succession, it seemed to the Ferrarist who was more interested in the road car evolved from the competition model that he might as well put behind him the old days. Manufacturers are not interested in the past. They have markets which have been researched and must plan their future models to fit them. While the engineer and coachwork designer are still important people in the world of the automobile they are certainly of less importance than the marketing men and auditors.

The ultimate shock to any die-hard came when the Paris Salon opened in October 1976. On the Ferrari stand was a model with automatic transmission – the 400 A – but there was also a manual version with a 5-speed transmission. The 400 A was equipped with a 3-speed General Motors Turbo-Hydromatic automatic transmission. In many respects the new model was similar to the 365 GT4 2 + 2 but with the engine enlarged to 4823cc. Pinin Farina designed and still builds the cars which are the most luxurious so far to come from Ferrari.

The V12 engine displaced 4823cc and the rated power was 340bhp at 6500rpm. By mid-1979 carburetors had been replaced with Bosch K-Jetronic fuel injection reducing the power output to 310bhp at 6400 rpm and a single Marelli distributor replaced the previous twin distributors. The limousine was now designated 400 GTi and 400ii Automatic. Included in the price was power steering and air conditioning. The interior was altered but not to any great extent but to give the whole a more up-market look. Perhaps one of the more significant alterations was to the rear suspension to give a smoother, more comfortable ride. Hydropneumatic self-leveling suspension has been incorporated, each piece of equipment working independently.

Above left: The 365 GTB 4 Daytona interior showed rear, early 1970s Italian design. Seating is apparently very comfortable and acceleration was breathtaking.

Left: Due to the many that were built later from coupes, the exact number of factory 365 GTS/4 is difficult to determine.

Above: The 4.4-liter V12 engine makes this 1971 365 GTS/4 a very desirable Ferrari indeed.

Right: The same 365 GTS 4. And the quality of the restoration work stands out a mile. From the paintwork to the beautifully retrimmed leather seats, every piece is as good as, if not better than, new.

Above: A 1973 246 GT Dino. Prices of cars like this have risen almost ten-fold over the last five years. The 246 was a development of the 206, recognizable by the 2418cc engine.

Left: By 1979, Ferrari had entered the big luxury car market with this 400i, the first production Ferrari ever offered with automatic transmission to back up the fuel-injected 4923cc V12.

Above right: The Spyder version of the 246 GT Dino was released in 1972 and each body was hand built at Scaglietti rather than on the usual 246 GT production line.

The V6 Gran Turismo cars

Up to 1957 Ferrari had built V12, in-line fours and in-line six cylinder cars but never a V6. In 1956 Vittorio Jano designed the first V6 unit and a number of formula 1 and 2 cars have been produced with such a configuration.

Ferrari had never dabbled in formula 1 racing to any great extent although he had been highly successful with the formula in the early days – first with the 166 F2 V12 and then with the in-line four 500 F2. But he was to have a go in 1967 when the FIA would be bringing in new regulations for formula 2. These stipulated that the maximum displacement would be 1600cc unsupercharged and engines with up to six cylinders would be permitted. To help keep the cost of the cars to a reasonable figure the FIA also decreed that the engines used had to be from a production series with a minimum of 500 units built within a twelve-month period.

As with other manufacturers Ferrari must have been feeling the financial strain since he was involved not only in formula 1 but also in GT and prototype racing. Apart from this he was only building highly sophisticated and exotic cars and although they were produced in reasonable numbers high priced Ferraris were not an everyday saleable commodity!

Ferrari was in a bit of a dilemma as he certainly had no facilities for building 500 engines in a twelve-month period if he wanted to enter the formula 2 stakes. The problem was finally resolved when Fiat agreed to produce Ing. Rocchi's V6 design although neither the independent Ferrari nor the non-racing Fiat factory were all that happy, but in the long run both were to benefit.

The run-up to the production Dino 206 GT were two sports prototypes – the 166 P and 206S. The first car was shown to the press and public at the Turin Show in 1967. While Pinin Farina designed the beautiful, sensual and flowing lines of the body he must have taken a hard look at Drogo's design for the 166 P and the exquisite 206 S. Before deciding on the ultimate shape. Pinin Farina had produced several designs including one with gull-wings and front and rear spoilers.

The 65-degree V6 unit was placed transversely behind the driving compartment. The 1987cc engine had twin camshafts per bank of cylinders, a single plug, coil ignition and three Weber 40 DCF carburetors. The 5-speed transmission was in unit with the differential. About 200 models were built by Scaglietti, all being berlinettas.

1969 was the year when Ferrari and Fiat joined forces and also the year when Ferrari put on show at Geneva his sensational Dino 246 GT which took the place of its smaller brother the 206 GT. The introduction of the model was probably Ferrari's answer to the smaller Porsche which was selling well and it was his intention to take a share of their market. The original price tag of $6000 made the car an attractive proposition, especially with the Ferrari connotation even if the badge on the nose and hub-caps proclaimed Dino and the script on the rear read Dino GT.

The 65-degree V12 engine was also placed transversely behind the driver's compartment. The engine was manufactured by Fiat and unlike Ferrari units, whose block castings were silumin, the 246 blocks were cast iron. Bodies were built by Scaglietti and while the dimensions were larger, including the overall height, the shape of the coachwork was more voluptuous without the flatness of its predecessor. The only trouble was that instead of using aluminum Scaglietti used steel which helped to add an unwanted 400lbs and affected the overall performance although a maximum top speed of 150mph was probably justified. In spite of the extra weight the Dino 246 GT was an extremely handy and maneuverable car on the road with few vices. The main complaint of owners of the early cars was a certain shoddiness in the interior, poor quality carpeting, lack of attention to detail, and poor fittings including the fittings of the bodywork panels, none of which was in the Ferrari tradition.

Three versions of the 246 were produced, the Type L (or Series I) with 357 examples built; the Type M (Series II), and with the introduction of the spyder, the Dino 246 GTS, in 1972 the Type E (Series III). This latter Type was introduced to comply with the stringent automobile legalities in force in the USA. The USA buyer also had a number of optional extras.

Overall there were probably in excess of 4000 models built and there can be no doubt that it was one of the best-selling cars the factory had designed even if many parts were of Fiat origin.

Left: Bertone's Dino 308 GT4 2+2 was the first regular production Ferrari since 1953 not designed by Pininfarina and never gained the following enjoyed by the 246 nor the other 308 models.

Below: The bright red carpet and restrained tan leather of a 308 GTB Quattrovalvole. Note the slender gear shifter.

Right: Many Ferrari enthusiasts considered the addition of fuel injection to the 308 GTB nothing short of sacrilege. Especially as it reduced power output by some 40bhp.

The V8 Gran Turismo cars

The V8 configuration was not a new departure for Ferrari as in the early sixties such units had been used for both grand prix and sports racing cars. However, it was a new concept for a road-going automobile from the factory.

The first V8 gran turismo model was seen at the Paris Salon in the fall of 1973 and was obviously to be the successor to the Dino 246 series. It was even designated Dino 308 GT4 2 + 2, which was a departure from Ferrari policy as it was thought that the appellation of Dino was exclusively for the V6 cars. Another surprise was that Ferrari had, for once, after many years, turned to Bertone to design the coachwork. To many who had grown to love the lines of Pinin Farina's designs it was a bit of a shock. Somehow the exotic Ferrari had been turned into a rather plain-looking car. It has to be admitted that attempting to give a 2 + 2 car flowing and sensuous lines has its difficulties especially when some headroom has to be found for the rear-seated passengers. So nobody should carp too much if the lines did not come up to what most expect from a Ferrari. Leaving out such criticism there can be no doubt that the performance and handling of the GT4 2 + 2 came up to expectations. While there might have been some sales resistance initially this has certainly been overcome since the model went out of production in 1980 as they are now sought after. Perhaps using the name 'Dino' was an error on the part of Ferrari. In any case three years after its introduction the name and badges were changed to Ferrari.

To comply with modern Ferrari practice the 90 degree V8 twin overhead camshaft per bank of cylinders engine was located transversely behind the center line of the car. So that a low-profile could be achieved at the rear the 5-speed synchromesh transmission was placed behind and not below the engine. Suspension, as with all Ferraris for many years, was fully independent, and to keep a smooth front line pop-up headlights were incorporated. The 2926cc engine was rated at 250bhp at 7700rpm.

Two years later the second 308 was introduced. This was the berlinetta 308 GTB, first seen in Paris and the body could only have come from Pinin Farina. It really was a masterpiece of design and the fluting from the doors blended into the side panels and ended in a not too large air scoop aperture. A central all-round indent was carried round the body. Sail planes from the roof were taken to the rear opening of the engine lid and the rear end was a Kamm-type cut-off. Five-spoke Campagnolo wheels added to the attractive lines and a small front spoiler enhanced the appearance. The engine was basically similar to the 308 GT4 2 + 2 but with dry-sump lubrication. The power rating was given as 255bhp at 7600rpm and the top speed in excess

of 150mph. The early cars were fiberglass but by mid-1977 the bodies were steel. All were and are built by Scaglietti. Also in 1977 the spyder or GTS version was shown at Frankfurt. It is always difficult to relate the word spyder to a berlinetta which has a portion of the roof removable so as to enjoy the 'passing' air – the term Targa would seem more appropriate. As with all cars with mid- or rear-mounted engines the question of baggage space arises. This is minimal, with some room under the hood but the main area is partitioned off behind the engine and while this might at first appear inadequate, quite a lot can be stowed away.

The overall performance is good all-round and was fit improved in 1981 when Bosch K-Jetronic fuel injection replaced the original four Weber 40 DCNF carburetors giving the 'new' car the designation 308 GTBi. Although the performance was good it was not good enough to out-perform some of the newer Porsches which, in turn, would mean a certain amount of sales resistance when a choice had to be made between the two marques. To improve this a four valve model was marketed in 1982 after the Mondial 8 had received the same treatment.

Previous pages: Like many of the later Ferrari Spyders, the 308 GTS was more of a Targa than a real Spyder. This is a US spec Quattrovalvole.

Left: First seen at the Geneva Show back in 1980, the Mondial 8 came as the replacement for the GT 4 2+2. The Cabriolet version came later.

Right: Although it matters little in this Cabriolet version, the Mondial was built on a long wheelbase chassis to allow the rear passengers proper adult headroom. The trim was all-leather with air-conditioning as standard. Even the luggage space is good for a Ferrari.

By 1980 the 308 GT4 2 + 2 was replaced by the Mondial 8 using the same power plant as the 308 series but located transversely as for the GT4 behind the rear seats. To give more rear passenger space the wheelbase was lengthened and the roof was raised by five inches. To add to the general interior spaciousness the overall width was increased by three inches. Because four adults could now be accommodated the luggage area was enlarged.

Styling was left to Pininfarina who did a far more satisfactory cosmetic job than Bertone, partly due to the greater overall length of the car. A small front spoiler gives an added refinement and the headlights are naturally of the pop-up variety. During 1982 the two valve per cylinder head was changed to a four-valve head and the engine received the same treatment as that of the 308 GTBi. Fiat or Ferrari changed the name by dropping the figure 8 and it became the Mondial quattrovalvole.

A number of changes have been made to the interior, the most notable being that made to the console over the central tunnel which now looks as though it has been designed into the car rather than placed in position as an afterthought. A number of detail changes have been carried out to instrumentation, and press buttons added, making for easier driving. The roof lining is a wool-type material fitted to the more expensive 512 BBi. Adjusting the outside mirrors has been made easier with the controls let into the driver's door and a Momo steering wheel has been included in the various improvements. The interior is, of course, upholstered in Connolly leather.

While there are still those who look back to the old days when a gran turismo was a thinly disguised racing car it has to be admitted that, under present-day driving conditions, the current production models are built for and can be used as commuter cars. They can also be used as daily transport for other purposes – including shopping.

At the 1984 Brussels show the Mondial became available as a graceful cabriolet, again following Pinin Farina designs and bodied by Scaglietti. Truly reawakening the image of the car as a proper Grand Tourer, it was a question of image rather than racebred performance. By now the racetrack was well and truly catered for in the shape of the GTO and the Testarossa, both of which had been shown in 1984 as well.

Then in 1985 came an increase in capacity up to 3195cc, and the two Mondials gained their 3.2 designations as well as a considerable boost in power – up from 214hp at 6600 rpm to 270 at 7000. Thus equipped, the Mondial could produce close to 150mph and reached 60mph from rest in slightly more than six seconds – more than acceptable performance from a car designed as an everyday car rather than a performance car. If any Ferrari can be considered for everyday use, that is. Interestingly, the Mondial was now built by Ferrari; increasingly – under the guiding hand of FIAT – the cars were built in-house and the Scaglietti name was gone.

The Fiat 12 (Boxer) Gran Turismo cars

The Ferrari flat 12 or boxer engine goes back to the 1964/65 seasons when the 1.5-liter 512 F1 was practiced by Bandini before the 1964 Italian Grand Prix held over the Monza circuit. It was some years before the flat 12 unit was used in a production gran turismo car. The first inkling that such a model was in the offing was at the 1971 Turin Show but production did not start until 1973 when the first 365 GT4/BB rolled out of the factory gates.

The 4390cc engine was mounted at the rear and had twin overhead camshafts, a single plug, coil ignition, and four Weber 40 IF3C carburetors. Pinin Farina designed the coachwork, Scaglietti built the main body parts of steel while the hood doors and the rear deck engine cover were aluminum. The lower body panels were fiberglass and were painted matt black. The styling was elegant and flowing, in contrast to the Daytona which it replaced.

In 1976 after a production run of nearly 390 units the model was replaced by the 512 BB. Some detail body changes were made to give the model its identity over its replacement. A narrow front spoiler was added and an air duct was included on the lower body panel ahead of the rear wheels and at the rear were four tail lamps instead of six.

The 512 BB (berlinetta boxer) has had many superlatives heaped upon it but in some respects its predecessor was its equal. The 512 BB had a power output of 340bhp at 6800rpm (the 365 GT4/BB was rated at 360bhp at 7500rpm). It would also seem that the 365 GT4/BB has been credited with a

maximum speed of 181mph whereas the current 512 BB has an estimated top speed of 174mph which is no higher than that claimed for the Daytona. Agreed that speed is not the ultimate criteria of a car's performance for other important factors have to be considered, but it does seem strange that what has been called a supercar can only muster the same speed as a car (the Daytona) which went out of production in 1973! The 12-cylinder luxury cars began life back in 1972 with the 365 GT4 2 + 2. The designation changed to 400 with the automatic 400i, and the latest to be shown was the 412, which appeared first at Geneva in 1985.

Basically similar to the 400i, the body (designed and built by Pinin Farina) reflected the growing aerodynamic trend and also from a V12 engine which now produced 340hp from 4942cc at 6000rpm. Torque is likewise boosted, and a new twin-plate clutch deals with the extra loads. And in keeping with its executive/touring/luxury status, the 412 has Bosch electronic ABS braking as a standard item, as well as electrically adjustable seats and electronically controlled airconditioning. Everyday items such as power steering and central door locking are also featured.

Ferrari Testarossa

It is fitting that at least the road cars were seen to be at their unassailable best when Enzo Ferrari died. Although on the track the fortunes of the Grand Prix team were most decidedly on the wane during his last years, Ferrari supremacy on the road seemed in an unchallengable position. And, though it was not the fastest Maranello road car of the late eighties, there can be no doubt whatsoever that the Testarossa is the car on which Ferrari's strength was founded.

Successor to the much-admired 512BB, the Testarossa is powered by the same four-cam flat 12 layout (although the engine was different inside). But its side-mounted radiators give it a dramatic extra width (a massive 78 ins) as well as its most prominent styling feature — those sweeping fins which run down its flanks.

The 512 was overdue for replacement, having been heavily revised since its launch at the 1971 Turin Show, and had in any case been totally overshadowed as the top performer in the Maranello range by the re-awakening of the GTO legend. As a development of the traditional Ferrari two-seat Berlinetta, with its engine ahead of the rear axle where it properly belonged in such a car, the Testarossa was the fastest of the normally-aspirated cars and was therefore perfectly positioned between road and race track.

Like the GTO, the Testarossa was named in honor of its famed V12 forerunners, and perhaps in the reappearance of both those names is a clue to the spirit of confidence which seemed to infect every corner of Maranello during the eighties. And perhaps a reawakened interest in sportscar racing; with the formula 1 fortunes decidedly on the wane from about 1983 (tragedians may even say that nothing really went right after the fateful 1982 season), it seemed perhaps significant that the new car should follow in the footsteps of the Testarossa which scored the first of six successive victories at Le Mans in 1960.

However there was nothing old-fashioned about the V12. Ferrari described it as the latest version of the V12 Boxer with four cams and four valves per cylinder used to win the formula 1 title in 1975, 1977, and 1979. Still perched above the transmission, as it had been in the 512, it had Bosch fuel injection and careful inlet manifold design to maximize the volumetric efficiency offered by its four-valve design, and it featured the latest word in microprocessor-controlled electronic ignition systems. That brought power up by 50hp to 390hp at 6800rpm, and also raised torque to 362lb ft at 4500rpm — 28lb ft better and 300rpm higher in the rev band.

Lighter than the 512BB by some 150lbs, the Testarossa makes no use of the new lightweight composite materials so prevalent in motor racing and

Previous pages: The Mondial 8 featured a 2926cc V8 with four cams, Bosch K-Jetronic ignition and Marelli Digiplex electronic ignition. The rev-limiter was set at 7500rpm, but it was still good for 140mph plus.

Left: With its bigger 4942cc flat-12 motor, the second series 512 BB is no slouch. But, with twin overhead cams per bank, dry sump and four triple-choke downdraft Webers, it jolly well shouldn't be.

Right: The 1984 Testarossa Show Car. As successor to the 512 BB, the Testarossa retained the four-cam flat-12, though it was modified to make it even faster.

Below: One of the most distinctive styling features of the eighties, the Testarossa's side fins allow for excellent cooling through the side-mounted radiators.

several of Ferrari's supercar competitors. And the same double unequal length wishbone layout is retained for its independent suspension.

But it isn't just the width that has gained some extra inches, the Testarossa is longer overall than the 512. It has a 2-inch growth in the wheelbase as well as a slightly wider track – although perhaps not as wide as its 5-inch gain in width might suggest.

Those side-mounted radiators have allowed Pininfarina to give the nose a lower, sharper profile and improve the overall aerodynamics of what is essentially a big car. Engine cooling is also better, and the trunk – at the front, of course – also gains useful extra space.

There is reputedly more space behind the seats for hand luggage, and there is definitely more headroom – an extra half-inch compared to the 512 – which answers a common criticism of what was essentially one of the best cars in the world.

Perhaps most remarkable of the styling changes introduced on the Testarossa, though not as obvious as the five strakes which cocoon the radiator intakes, is the final farewell to the twin rear light configuration which had been a Ferrari hallmark for so long. The two red lights are gone, replaced by wraparound oblongs hiding inside an extended rear grille.

Though they retained the characteristic flavor, the five-spoke alloy wheels too were new, 16 inches in diameter and perhaps under-tired with the same 225/50 and 255/50 Goodyear VRs as the 512.

The criticisms of the tires voiced by some testers once the honeymoon period had ended were perhaps prompted by the late eighties habit of applying larger and larger tires to road cars, perhaps by the fact that with its extra power and reduced weight, the Testarossa was markedly quicker than the 512. Top speed was claimed at 181mph in European (non-catalyser) trim, though few road testers ever saw this number on the speedometer.

Acceleration was definitely better – Maranello said the 0-100kph (62.5mph) time was 5.8 seconds, half a second faster than the 512. Most magazine road testers gave the Testarossa 0-60mph times in the region of 5.2 or 5.3 seconds, depending on weather and track, and put the failure to reach an indicated 181mph down to tire scrub on the banked test circuits. After all, there are few roads which will permit sustained straight-line cruising at 180mph under controlled conditions.

Fuel consumption under hard-driving road conditions produced fairly acceptable 16/17 mpg – well below the gas-guzzler threshold, but certainly tolerable to anyone prepared to part with more than $93,000 to buy the car in the first place.

Above: Presently changing hands for quite substantially more than the factory asking price, the Testarossa looks set to become one more Ferrari that will be coveted by car collectors the world over.

Left: A low, laid-back driving position, is just the job for cruising at Testarossa's top speed of 181mph. Or getting you to 60mph in 5.2 seconds, come to that.

Index

Page numbers in *italics* refer to illustrations

Acknowledgments

The publisher would like to thank David Eldred the designer, Maria Costantino the picture researcher, Clive Prew for writing the captions, Ron Watson for preparing the index, and the individuals and agencies listed below for providing the illustrations:

Neill Bruce Photographic: pages 8(right), 12(both), 14-15, 17(both), 22, 27(below), 28-29, 32, 34, 35(top), 36-37, 38(both), 39(both), 40, 43(below), 50, 51, 52, 53(both), 54(top), 56, 57(top), 58-59, 60(both), 61, 62(both), 63(both), 64(top), 65, 70(both), 71, 78, 80(All 3), 81(top), 95, 107(below), 109(both), 110, 111, 112(top), 113(both), 114(below), 115, 116(both), 117, 120, 121, 122-123, 125(both), 126(both)
Geoffrey Goddard: pages 6-7, 8(left), 16, 19, 20(top & main picture),23(below), 24, 26, 31, 33,

35(below), 57(below), 72-73, 74,75(below), 79(both), 81(below), 82, 83(below), 85(both), 86, 87(top), 88, 89(top), 90, 91(both), 93(below), 94, 100(top)
Haymarket Publishing: pages 93(top), 107(top)
Andrew Morland: pages 11, 13, 66, 77(both)
Don Morley: pages 83(top), 84(both), 96, 97(below), 98(both), 99
National Motor Museum, Beaulieu: pages 68-69, 100(below), 101(below left & right), 102, 103(both), 106, 114(top), 124
National Motor Museum, Beaulieu/ Nicky Wright: pages 10, 21(top), 23(top), 27(top), 30, 41, 42, 43(top), 44-45, 46, 47, 48 49(both), 54(below), 75(top), 76, 87(below), 89(below), 108, 112(below)
Quadrant Picture Library: pages 92, 97(top), 101(top)
The Research House: pages 64(below), 104-105, 118-119